W9-AUI-496

Fat, Forty, and Fired

Fat, Forty, and Fired

One Man's Frank, Funny, and Inspiring
Account of Losing His Job and
Finding His Life

Nigel Marsh

Andrews McMeel
Publishing, LLC
Kansas City

07 08 09 10 11 RR4 10 9 8 7 6 5 4 3 2 1

Library of Congress Cataloging-in-Publication Data

Marsh, Nigel, 1964–
    Fat, forty, and fired : one man's frank, funny, and inspiring account of losing his job and finding his life / Nigel Marsh.
        p. cm.
    Originally published: Sydney : Bantam, 2005.
    ISBN-13: 978-0-7407-6433-2
    ISBN-10: 0-7407-6433-0
        1. Marsh, Nigel, 1964– 2. Middle-aged men—Australia—Biography. 3. Fathers—Australia—Biography. 4. Househusbands—Australia—Biography. 5. Advertising executives—Australia—Biography. 6. Unemployed—Australia—Biography. 7. Life change events. I. Title.

HQ1059.5.A8M37 2007
305.244'10994—dc22

                                                                                    2006047951

www.andrewsmcmeel.com

First published in Australia and New Zealand in 2005 by Bantam

Cover design by Darian Causby/Highway 51
Cover candle compliments of Boston Warehouse, Norwood, Massachusetts

Pages 260–61: "The Bad Touch," words and music by James Franks. Copyright © 2000 by Songs of Polygram/Hey Rudy Music/Jimmy Franks Music, Universal Music Publishing P/L. Printed with permission. All rights reserved.

Page 267: Extract from "Balance Is Bunk!" by Keith Hammonds, copyright © 2005 by Gruner & Jahr USA Publishing. First published in *Fast Company* magazine. Reprinted with permission.

For Kate, Alex, Harry, Grace, and Eve.
Always have, always will.

Introduction

DO YOU EVER FANTASIZE about moving to the country or a beach and downsizing? If so I know how you feel. I've spent the last two decades slogging my guts out in a variety of different jobs, for the most part in a decidedly rainy, urbanized country.

Like most of the population, when I started I had no assets to fall back on or family influence to gain leverage in any particular field for a smooth entry into the workplace. More important, I had no money beyond that which I could earn each week. London can be a pretty unforgiving place for a young man with no connections or qualifications beyond being able to read the Bible in Greek and a valid driver's license.

The early signs after I finished my education and moved to the city to seek my fortune weren't particularly encouraging. But I didn't have a family to look after, and sleeping in a mate's car while working on the railway didn't seem all that bad at the time.

As the years passed, I eventually secured a foothold on the bottom rung of a career ladder that seemed to suit my particular talents— the world of marketing beckoned. My progress up the greasy pole was satisfactory, and I soon found myself above the poverty line. Indeed, after a few years I even qualified for the dizzying heights of middle management.

My personal responsibilities—four kids and counting—grew, along with my earning power, the former nicely canceling out the potential benefits of the latter. I began to work harder and harder to stay afloat. I changed jobs, companies—even countries—to further my career. As the years went by, though, I began to be aware of an increasingly persistent voice in my head. *What's it all for, Nige? Your life is slipping away. You need to change your priorities and spend proper time with your family.* The voice wouldn't go away; indeed it just got louder as time passed. Of course for a long time I didn't change my lifestyle or take time off, but that didn't stop me from spending the last ten years having escapist daydreams about kicking it all in.

Then, in 2003, I found myself downsized and living in Sydney, Australia. The reality didn't quite match the dream. According to a recent headline in the *Financial Times,* "Poor is the new rich and dropping out is the dream." Bullshit. Poor is poor and dropping out can be a nightmare.

I haven't got a catchy slogan that sums up what I learned from my year off. I do know, however, that men aren't from Mars and fat isn't a feminist issue. Men are from Earth and fat is fat. I don't claim to have usable wisdom for anyone else. All I can say is that I lived the dream of dropping out for a year and this is how it was for me.

Chapter 1

Paper Pants

SANTA DIDN'T COME to Sydney last year. The community nurse came instead. My four kids weren't exactly thrilled with this swap—but then again, neither was I. Having over two pounds of seaweed gauze repeatedly packed into a fresh-cut ass wound does tend to take the edge off one's festive mood. Particularly when your company is about to be merged out of existence and you are stuck halfway around the world, fifteen thousand or so miles away from family and home back in England.

But worse things have happened at sea, as my dad always says. I'm damned if I know why worse things happening at sea is supposed to help, but it's the sort of useless counsel you seem to get when your life's in the toilet and people are trying to be kind. I was just going to have to put into practice some of the advice

I'd gleaned from the covers of those self-help books you see in airports to help me deal with the problem.

The problem had reared its head precisely a week before. A visit to my doctor with what I thought was a boil on my butt resulted in me being told to put a green gown on backward and sign a lot of forms absolving anyone from blame if I were to die. An "anal fistula" is the correct medical term for my early Christmas present—Henry V died of one at age thirty-six—and a fistulectomy is the operation. (The postoperation packing process itself hasn't got an official medical term, as they couldn't translate "godawfulsustainedpainandmisery" into Latin.) Twelve hours later I woke up after such an operation in Sydney's Prince of Wales Hospital to groggily tell my wife, Kate, "That wasn't so bad."

"The surgery is the easy bit. It's the packing that's the killer," the doctor rather too cheerfully corrected me. Leaving aside the fact that at this point I didn't know what "packing" was, all I could think was, "How bad can that be?" As it turns out, badder than bad. Not just tear-jerkingly, painfully bad, but soul-destroyingly, humiliatingly bad. The first nurse who performed this task on me was delightful, empathetic, and skilled. She barely batted an eyelid as I screamed like a woman in the final stages of labor.

"There. All done, Mr. Marsh," she said.

"Oh, thanks so much and sorry for all the noise. At least the worst is over now. I don't think I could face ever having to do that again." She then gently explained that someone would have to do it every day for at least six weeks.

"Every day?" I groaned.

"Every day," she confirmed.

"Christmas Day?"

"Christmas Day."

"New Year's Day?"

"New Year's Day."

At which point I adopted the role of Scrooge, not Santa, and effectively destroyed any festive spirit. I soon forgot the airport self-help books and settled into a marriage-wrecking combination of self-pity, anger, and helplessness. "Daddy's cranky" was how Alex, my gorgeous seven-year-old, put it to all our rejected Christmas well-wishers.

Matters weren't helped by the fact that it was a different nurse who came to perform the packing almost every day. Having a succession of complete strangers (two of whom were males) come into your bedroom, move your nuts to one side, and fiddle with your ass every day takes its toll on your dignity. On Boxing Day, in a bid to arrest my slide into total despair, I announced to my rightly cynical wife that I wouldn't remain bedridden by this minor mishap. "We're all going to the beach," I barked. However, my newfound lust for life was short-lived.

"Kate, I've lost it," I snapped, as I gingerly stepped onto the sand.

"Lost what?" my wife good-naturedly replied.

"My pad. The goddamn panty pad has gone." Somewhere on the walk between our house and the beach, the panty pad I had to wear over my wound had fallen out of my paper hospital pants.

A radical reappraisal was clearly needed.

Chapter 2

Brainfrog

AS LUCK WOULD have it, the timing was perfect for a reappraisal. A few weeks prior to my butt problems I had received a phone call telling me that our worldwide holding company was to merge with another. No biggie, I thought, it happens all the time. Then my boss went on to explain that one of the end results of this process was that the firm I was running in Australia would have to close—or, more accurately, I would have to close it. Given that my partners and I had just devoted a year of our lives building it into something of a success, this was less than welcome news. It would inevitably mean many colleagues—none of whom had done anything wrong—would lose their jobs.

We had become a very close-knit, ferociously loyal team, and this prospect made me feel enormously sad—as well as guilty. I don't care what they teach you at business school; I view the primary role of any CEO as providing meaningful employment, not taking it away. Any idiot can cut costs; it's building something valuable (in all the senses of that word) that's the real challenge.

As a desperate measure I wrote to the new ultimate boss in Paris, offering to buy the local company from him. To make a long story short, the answer was *non*. In a cynical business such as advertising it is easy to mock a group of people who claim to believe in a common goal beyond naked self-interest, but that is precisely what we had at D'Arcy Australia. The company was more than an economic trading unit of an international firm; it was family. Unfortunately, it really did look like the family was coming to an end. And as the head of that family, I was ashamed of my failure. I was also exhausted and out of balance. Attempting to look after one family had led me to grievously neglect the other.

The one upside of having to lie on your stomach for two weeks is that it gives you time to think. The more I thought about it, the more I wanted a change. I'd recently read a book called *Manhood,* by a chap named Steven Biddulph, that argued that every man should be forced to take his fortieth year off. His theory was that the vast majority of men don't have a life—they pretend to have one. In reality they are lonely, emotionally timid, and miserably, compulsively competitive.

One of the main reasons they never escape this tragic state is that they are enslaved by soulless jobs and careers that lead them to put their lives on hold until retirement. Of course, when this arrives it is too late. While they work they are too busy to think, and therefore they have empty lives because they never develop a rich and sustaining inner life. As Biddulph himself puts it, "Our marriages fail, our kids hate us, we die of stress, and on the way we destroy the world." I wasn't sure if it was the effects of the medication I was on, but his year-off notion struck a real chord. Besides, while I wasn't being forced—I could have looked for a new job—circumstances were rather suited to a pause for reflection and a change of direction.

For a while now I had had the nagging feeling that all my glories were former glories. As my riches had increased, my "interest factor" had decreased. As a young man I used to have a vibrant social life both inside and outside of work. I don't want to pretend I was a culture vulture, but it would be fair to say I had the skill of burning the candle at both ends down to a fine art.

Every night was like its own miniature weekend. Live music, stand-up comedy, nightclubs, or just plain boozing was the standard fare Monday to Friday. Come the real weekends it got more adventurous as sports, trips away, and two-day parties got thrown into the mix. Irrespective of how immature and irresponsible I was, the one thing my life wasn't was one-dimensional. Now I only seemed to work, prepare for work, complain about work, or go to sleep—and dream about work.

Also, more worryingly, my "nice factor" was diminishing. I was sure all parents shouted at their kids, but I was less certain they shouted at them quite as often as I did. I'd become a bit player in my family—leaving in the morning before they got up and arriving home after they were in bed (but early enough, unfortunately, to catch Kate and bore her to tears with yet more dull stories of my work travails). And I was concerned that my four-year-old, Harry, had started to exhibit some bizarre character traits. We only noticed these when one of his pictures came back from preschool signed "Batbounce." Kate and I thought little of this until the next piece of artwork came back with "Brainfrog" written neatly in the corner.

Kate was equally nonplussed by this behavior, so I decided to take matters into my own hands. I arranged to pick Harry up from his school. Rather embarrassingly, this involved getting directions from Kate, as it was a task I'd never performed before. Having eventually found the correct street, I parked the car, signed myself in at the preschool door as the "pick-up parent," and went in search of the person in charge. Pick-up time is mayhem and not the best time to be a worried parent demanding reassurance and attention, but Harry's teacher couldn't have been nicer when I located her.

"Excuse me, I'm Harry's dad. He brought back some pictures with strange names on them last week and I wondered what the purpose of this practice is," I asked his teacher.

"Oh no, Mr. Marsh, it is not a school practice," she replied. "It's just that for the last few months Harry has come into class each morning and announced his name is not Harry, told us his new name—Spiderpotter, Winnie Ranger, Brainfrog, things like that—and then refused to answer to any other name."

"Did you say a few months?" I asked.

"Yes, we assumed you were playing along with it at home."

I tortured myself all week long with increasingly awful scenarios of what this behavior might actually mean. Was it reflective of deep-seated personality problems that I had given the young mite by being a lousy dad? Had my impatience and shouting led him to invent an imaginary set of personalities who enabled him to escape into a nicer world? It was all but impossible to stop this self-flagellating mind chatter—until, of course, the weekend, which I spent shouting at him and his brother and sisters as usual.

Whether or not Harry's name games had anything to do with me, it was clear I had lost perspective. Work had become a far too dominant factor in my life and I was becoming that person I always swore I would never be—an office rat who lived to work, not worked to live. In this case, the problem was compounded by the fact that the work was out of sync with my personal values and motivations. So not only was I spending too little time with my family, but the rare time I was with them was being ruined by my grumpy, conflicted, and jaded demeanor.

Advertising is one of those professions that from the outside can often be seen as terribly glamorous. The truth rarely—if ever—lives up to the myth. The industry has long since had its heyday. Advertising agencies no longer pay well or offer an attractive working life full of long lunches and end-of-year bonuses. If you run an agency you not only have to deal on a daily basis with a long list of ever more demanding clients, but you often have to convince exhausted and underpaid employees to work unreasonable hours for precious little reward. Ten or so fourteen-hour days in a row, a key client defection, and a couple of unwanted resignations, topped off nicely by a call from your boss complaining about the firm's lack of double-digit growth, can make you a very irritable and dull boy indeed.

Trouble was, the nastier I became, the nicer my family was. It would have been some comfort if I had a shrew for a wife and revolting, unlikable children, but the reverse was the case. Kate and I had been married for ten years, during which time she had been nothing but supportive and understanding. Along the way she had sacrificed her career and given me four of the most gorgeous children that ever walked the earth.

Alex, Harry, and Grace and Eve, our three-year-old twins, created a tidal wave of loving welcome every time I came home after work. The moment they heard my key in the door they would leap up from whatever they were doing (to Kate's understandable irritation if it was dinnertime) and hurtle down the corridor toward the front door, all shouting, "Daddy! Daddy! Daddy's home!" As they progressed down the hall they would become one interwoven child with eight arms and eight legs. More often than not, they would bang headlong into the door before I had opened it, their combined force making it impossible for me to push it open. Kate would have to peel them away to enable me to squeeze in and receive the breathless daily offering of drawings, paintings, and sports results.

A luckier man has never existed, yet increasingly I was responding to this unquestioning barrage of love with a grunt, or worse, a curt flash of anger. On some occasions, after driving home from work I was so spent that I found myself staying in the car listening to the radio rather than going inside. In my more rational moments I would berate myself for this behavior and sink despairingly into a sea of self-loathing, but mainly I just unthinkingly trampled all over the feelings of those who meant the most to me. And then I was informed of the forthcoming closure of my firm.

In early December I took a long flight to New York to meet Hank, the big cheese of our international company. I had been prepared for the meeting for a number of weeks, ever since it was announced that all our firm's offices around the world were going to be merged. In these situations, the first person to get the ax is the guy who runs the firm that is going to be merged—in this case, me—so I was expecting the worst. I traveled straight from JFK airport to the skyscraper that housed our corporate headquarters. The offices were impressive—all marble and glass. I was ushered to the thirty-third floor and into the waiting room outside Hank's office.

For a man who ran a large global corporation, Hank was pleasantly informal and open.

"Hi, Nigel, good to see you. How was your flight? Can I get Dani to get you a coffee? Water?" he asked when I was summoned into his enormous corner office with stunning views of Central Park.

In return I asked him how he was and he spoke candidly about his year. How difficult it had been. How everyone was out to get him. How disappointing the situation was. *Hold on,* I thought. *Aren't you the guy who has just personally pocketed $85 million as a result of the merger deal? Kate and I could handle a disappointment like that.* I bit my tongue and said nothing.

He went on.

And on.

And on.

It was fifty-five minutes into the meeting and he hadn't mentioned Australia, let alone me. We were still on how much traveling he had to do, how hurtful the press was being about his personal earnings from the deal, and how tough it was dealing with the investor community.

I started to doubt if he knew who I was. Perhaps he was playing for time, hoping someone would remind him. I thought I'd help him out.

"Must have been awful for you, I can only imagine," I said. "Sounds like you've weathered the storm remarkably well though, Hank. We could do with some of your know-how in Australia," I added, pointedly.

"Ah, Australia," he replied, visibly perking up. "Do you still have that harbor?"

"Harbor?"

"Yes, harbor. Sydney Harbor."

"Yes, we still have it," I replied. *Is it the jet lag or are we actually talking complete and utter bullshit,* I found myself wondering. *I've flown fourteen thousand miles to be made redundant and after an hour all we are doing is a slightly retarded geographical trip down memory lane.*

I decided to raise the issue myself.

"With the proposed merger, I was wondering what counsel you would give me personally," I asked.

"My advice to you is to get a seat on the bus—any seat, any bus—just get one and sit on it," he replied, with surprising and forceful conviction. I couldn't help thinking of that scene in *The Graduate* when Dustin Hoffman is ushered outside at a party to receive some deadly serious career advice, only to be told the single word "plastics."

Hank went on to explain laboriously that it was an analogy (no shit, Sherlock) and that in any merger the prime purpose for someone like me was to secure a job at all costs, irrespective of role or location. He didn't mention personal hopes or aspirations. Corporate vision didn't get brought up either. Remain employed or else was the simple message. He was eager and seemed genuine in his desire to help toward this end. The meeting ended with him recommending a couple of people he thought I should see who had positions they would like to talk to me about. It seemed picky to point out that both the roles in question were based in the Northern Hemisphere and I had only twelve months earlier moved my entire family to the Southern Hemisphere. Instead, I thanked him for his time and promised that I would give serious thought to his advice.

Which is exactly what I did. The meeting might have been slightly bizarre, but it definitely helped me decide what to do. Hank's viewpoint wasn't unusual and, from a certain perspective, his advice was completely correct. However, from another perspective it's bloody stupid to get on a bus if you don't like where it's going. Not only did I not want to screw up my own life, I wanted to set the right example for my kids. At the risk of stretching the metaphor to death, I wanted them to know that sometimes it might be better to slow down and walk to places instead of being on a bus driven by someone else. You get to choose the route and you could end up learning more. If it all goes wrong, you can always get on another bus.

I couldn't help thinking it was time to take the plunge and take a break from the corporate world. You are a long time dead, and I'd always doubted that sitting in an office was the sum of all the world has to offer. Besides, I'd never regretted any previous risk I had taken, be it doing stand-up comedy, moving to Australia, studying theology, or going for baby number three, which turned out to be twins. In fact, far from being the "silly" bits of my life, these risks had invariably been the things that made me feel alive and supplied me with the memories I most cherished. Perhaps a year off the treadmill was precisely what I, and my family, needed.

The more I thought about it, the more attractive the option appeared. An article in the newspaper gave me added encouragement. It quoted a statistic from a recent survey stating that 88 percent of Australians are dissatisfied with their work and are looking for a more meaningful and balanced life. Perhaps I wasn't so unusual after all.

I began to fantasize in an entirely unrealistic way about all the things I could do if I didn't have to go to the goddamn office. Apparently most people overestimate what they can do in a year and underestimate what they can do in ten. I don't know about the ten-year bit, but I can testify to suffering from chronic self-delusion in the twelve-months part. My list started with the usual weight-loss and fitness goals. After a couple of beers I added learning to speak Russian and drawing regularly. A couple more and I was educating the kids at home and running for mayor. By the time I had finished the six-pack I'd moved on to world peace and a cure for cancer. I only realized I was in la-la land when "winning Wimbledon for Britain" appeared on the list. After all, there are some things that are never going to happen.

Chapter 3

Lamb or Swordfish

SELF-CENTERED THOUGH I may be, I realized that dropping out wasn't a decision I should take lightly—or alone. I clearly needed a proper discussion with Kate before doing anything rash. I took the momentous step of booking a restaurant for dinner for the night after my return. I say momentous because although dinner out in a nice restaurant with Kate is one of the greatest pleasures of my life, it is also one of the most frustrating activities I have ever experienced. Throughout our marriage I have come to dread the never-changing opening scenario involved when Kate and I eat out together. It's not that Kate isn't good company—she is. It's not that we don't like the same places—we do. It is simply that she makes the ordering process mind-numbingly, soul-crushingly painful. In fact, she's made it an art form.

The conversation always starts in the same way. This night was clearly going to be no exception.

"Have you chosen?" she asked, after we'd studied the menus for a couple of minutes.

"Yep," I replied.

"What are you having?"

"Think I'll go with the swordfish tonight."

"Are you sure?" she probed.

Oh my God, here we go.

"Yep," I replied.

"Why?"

"Christ, I don't know. I just fancy it."

Kate beckoned the waiter over.

"What do you recommend?" she asked him.

"It's all good, madam."

Oh shit, the worst answer. *We're in for the full reduce-me-to-tears version tonight,* I thought as Kate replied, "Yes, but what would you have?"

"Er . . . I usually have the lamb or the swordfish, madam."

"Is the lamb nice?"

"Nice?"

"Yes, nice. Is it good? Do you think I would like it? I'm not sure I'm in the mood for anything heavy."

"Then I think the swordfish would be perfect for you, madam."

You think you're clever, mate, but you're out of your depth. No one gets away that easily.

"No, I can't have the swordfish, because that would mean we're both having it."

"That's all right, sweetheart, I don't mind," I said.

"But that's no fun—both having the same thing."

"Actually, I've changed my mind. I'll have the lamb," I said to the waiter, who looked strangely like he wanted to hug me.

"No. You're just saying that. You stick with the fish. I'll have something else," Kate said.

I was losing the will to live and we were now no nearer a decision than we had been five minutes before.

"What are they having?" Kate inquired, pointing to the next table.

"That's the soup of the day, madam—a very nice light starter," the waiter replied.

"Could I have it as a main?" Kate asked.

Much more of this and you'll be wearing it as a hat, I thought. I could go on—she did—but I'll spare you. Needless to say, I lost my temper, we had an argument, I forced her into a decision, she sulked, and we sat in silence, broken in the traditional way by Kate when our meals arrived.

"Yours looks good. I wish I'd ordered the swordfish," she said.

That's not to say we didn't have the chat we intended to. In fact it was easier talking about what to do with the rest of our lives than it was ordering the damn food.

"I think I want to take a year off," I started.

"You mean they haven't offered you a job you want?" she replied.

"Fair comment. I'm not excited by anything they've offered. But I think it's more than that. I want a life change."

"To do what?"

"Don't know. Nothing. Not put a tie on. Get to know my kids properly. Be a real part of the family. Find a positive outlet other than a traditional career."

"But how would we earn money?" Kate asked.

"We wouldn't," I replied.

"Then how would we live?"

"Off our savings." Kate raised her eyebrows quizzically and lit a cigarette before getting to the heart of the matter.

"How long would that last?" she asked.

"If we were sensible, it could last for a year," I replied.

"What type of sensible?" Kate asked.

"Well, we'd have to move to a smaller house. And sell the Subaru. And the nanny would have to go. Apart from that, not much would have to change."

"And what would happen at the end of the year?" Damn, exactly the question I'd been hoping she wouldn't ask.

"Honestly?" I replied.

"Honestly."

"We'd be screwed. All our savings would be gone. I'd be a forgotten, forty-year-old advertising executive who hadn't worked for a year. Unemployable."

"So I get twice the husband, half the income, and at the end of the year we'll both have to work at Wal-Mart?"

"Basically."

Kate thought for a minute. "If we do this, will you be less of an asshole?"

"That's the reason I'd be doing it. I can't promise, but I'll try."

Kate reached over and took a bite of my swordfish. She chewed thoughtfully, then smiled at me.

"Well, I'm up for it if you think it will make you happy."

If only she was this decisive when choosing a main course.

Chapter 4

Little Lunch

AFTER I RETURNED from fistula leave, I still had a month at my old job to finally make up my mind about the future. Merging a company isn't exactly a barrel of laughs, but it was extremely important to me to do it as well as I could, right up until the very end. Not just out of professional pride, but because as CEO, my actions would mean the difference between others losing or keeping their jobs. Just because I was more than likely going to chuck it all didn't mean others had the desire or the means not to work. Everyone whom I had worked with so far in Australia had been incredibly fair, and I wanted to pay them back by getting them jobs in the new firm or looking after them as generously as I could.

Having said that, winding up a company is a different day-to-day existence from running it, so I had more time on my hands.

Kate and I were determined that we would use that time to extend my working knowledge of the new life I was thinking of signing up for. Our reasoning was that I would be better able to make the final decision to leave the workplace if I had tasted a few of the delights in store for me on the other side. We set upon January 31 as the date when we would finally commit either way.

We started the experiment gently with an easy assignment. I was to take the morning off and do the school run. Not for all the kids, but just for the boys. This would involve taking Alex to school and Harry to preschool. I was terrified of performing this task but wanted to prove to myself that I could do it—after all it was a new, improved, "balanced" life I was thinking of embarking on. Kate was taking the bus with the girls to something called Kindi Gym and I'd be driving the boys.

I set the alarm early. *The more time, the better,* I thought, since even I knew there is nothing like a deadline and children to get the shouting going. But despite my lack of experience, the kids' truculence, and my hangover from dinner, after an hour's feverish activity I was immensely proud to have both the little buggers in the car. Admittedly Alex was wearing Harry's top and Harry had on his sister's shoes, but they were in the car, and Alex had a packed lunch made for him entirely by his dad.

It had taken over an hour of tears, shouting, and whining to get the right combination of peanut butter, banana, apple juice, and chips sorted out but it was 8:45, the car was running, and I had a full fifteen minutes to get Alex to school and then another fifteen to drive on with Harry to preschool. The traffic, however, was a nightmare. It seemed to take forever as we inched toward the school. Finding a parking spot was just as bad. My already high anxiety levels began to soar. I was still determined we wouldn't be late if at all possible. By then I was liberally cursing under my breath and strangling the steering wheel with a white-knuckled grip. I simply couldn't see anywhere to park the car. In desperation I pulled up illegally right outside the school gates. Three minutes to go. We'd make it if we hurried.

"Open the door, Alex, open the door, Alex, OPEN THE DOOR. Oh for Christ's sake, I'll do it."

I slid the side door open and watched as Alex's school bag fell out of the car onto the pavement and his favorite Clovelly Rugby Club drink bottle dropped out of its top pocket and, in slow motion, rolled into the drain and was washed out of sight.

"Don't cry, sweetheart—Harry, open the door—I'll get you another one, Alex. Harry, open the door—come on, Alex, the bell's about to go. Oh for Christ's sake, Harry, I'll do it."

I ran around to the other side of the car, only to have my progress violently halted by the edge of the don't park here, school children crossing sign embedding itself in my left eyebrow.

"Jesus friggin' Christ," I screamed, immediately dropping to my knees. A local mom tutted loudly at my language in front of my—and her—kids. Another, more sympathetic mom came over to say, "You're bleeding, dear. Are you all right?" As she helped me to my feet, she politely asked why Alex had a packed lunch when it was cafeteria day.

"Cafeteria day?" I replied weakly. "What's that?"

"It's the day once a week when parents bring in money for the lunch room and no packed lunches are allowed."

"Where's the cafeteria?" I asked.

"Over there, but you better hurry, orders close at nine o'clock."

I didn't feel well enough to shout at anyone, so I simply dragged my sons to the counter. Amazingly, the $3.30 I had in small change—I hadn't brought any bills—just covered my hurried order for one lunch. "Little lunch," however, was a different matter, pushing my budget and my temper over the edge.

"What's little lunch?" I asked the cafeteria lady.

"It's the favorite part of the day for most kids," she replied. "It's when the important bonding happens. All the kids gather outside on the basketball court at 10:20 and have a snack. The ritual swapping of sweets, chips, and the like is quite fascinating. Most kids would rather go to school with no trousers on than have no little lunch." This last unhelpful bit of information was said with a pitying glance at Alex.

Five minutes before, I'd never heard of little lunch, let alone known what it was, yet now it was single-handedly ruining my entire life. I felt bad enough for making Alex move schools and countries at the tender age of six, but here I was making it impossible for him to fit in because I didn't know the first thing about how his school worked.

I presented my by now miserable little-lunchless son to his class teacher with a muttered, "Sorry he's late," before driving Harry to preschool while clutching a cafeteria napkin to my still-bleeding eye. We didn't say a word on the journey—so much for quality time with my kids. I'd had visions of a relaxed breakfast, joking together in the car, and then running around on the playground. Instead I had spent the entire time stomping around underneath my own personal storm cloud. I felt guilty, stressed, and inadequate. I dropped Harry off and then took the opportunity to stroll down the hill to the local beach café for a soothing morning coffee.

I sat in the window seat and tried to relax myself by looking at the view of the waves gently rolling onto Bronte beach. It was a pleasant spot and, sure enough, five minutes later I was starting to feel a little better. I ordered a second coffee and had just sat down again when our next-door neighbor, who also had a child at the preschool, walked past the window, noticed me, and came in to say hello.

"Morning, Nigel, what are you doing here?" she asked.

"I'm taking the morning off work. I've just dropped Harry off at preschool," I replied.

"Oh, isn't he cute. I simply love the way he stands at the Good-bye Window."

"The Good-bye Window?"

"Yes, the way he stands on his school bag so he can reach the sill to kiss his mom—or obviously today his dad—good-bye before he'll agree to join the others."

My heart lurched. I excused myself from the conversation and ran as fast as I could back up the hill to the preschool.

"Where's the Good-bye Window?" I panted to a mother who was just leaving.

"Over there. It's the one with the blond boy leaning on the sill," she said, pointing toward my younger son.

As I approached the window I could see there were tears rolling down Harry's cheeks.

"Daddy, I waited. Where were you?" he asked in a trembling, bewildered voice.

I can't actually find the words to describe how I felt. I hated myself and loved him with equal passion. How could I be such a useless idiot? I only had to do the school run, something Kate managed every day, and I'd completely screwed it up. I imagined Harry being interviewed in prison in later life, telling a sympathetic Oprah Winfrey, "I decided to turn to violent crime after my father left me weeping in front of my classmates so he could get himself a coffee . . ."

This is so hard, I thought as I drove home. Little lunch, Good-bye Windows—what other unknown obstacles were out there waiting to trip me up? I parked outside the house and trudged inside. Kate was sitting in the garden sipping a to-go latte, looking radiant and relaxed.

"Hi, sweetheart, how were the lads?"

"Fine," I lied.

"Excellent. Well, now you've done it once, I thought next time you'd like to do it properly and take the girls as well as the boys."

I couldn't help wondering if the bus still had some seats left on it.

Chapter 5

Kindi Gym

A WEEK AFTER MY disastrous trip with the boys, I took another morning off work to try the school run again. Given my previous experiences I approached this event with some trepidation. Luckily Kate relented on the four-kids-at-once challenge and instead gave me the girls' Kindi Gym trip to do.

Grace and Eve are identical twins. We hadn't planned on having four kids, but in retrospect I feel blessed that we were given this particular parenting experience. Half the time they looked like one child with four big trusting eyes and one enormous mop of blond hair. Until a year before they had actually slept in the same bed with their faces pressed together like two interlocked jigsaw pieces. Both Kate and I still sometimes mistook one for the other, and other people did all the time. Harry identified them simply by pointing and saying "That one hit me" or "The one with the hat on needs the bathroom."

Grace has a small mole on the side of her neck and became so used to having people look for it to establish who was who that now if anyone said, "What's your name?" she automatically lifted up her hair and pointed to her mole. This was understandably disconcerting when she wasn't actually with Eve and the person asking didn't know she had a twin. On one slightly worrying occasion, a kindly old lady in the local park asked Eve her name. Eve shocked Kate by replying, "I'm Graceandeve."

The twins were best friends in a way that made my heart melt, walking around holding hands, hugging each other if one was upset and needed comforting. On top of how they looked, they also sounded cute. Their accents were a unique blend of English, Australian, South African, German, Scottish, and Canadian— the nationalities of all the nannies we had been lucky to have over the years.

Although they looked and sounded the same, Grace and Eve had certain distinguishing character traits, food being one of them. Eve could take it or leave it, while Grace had yet to make the link between hunger and food. She simply thought if it was put in front of you, you ate it. Whenever Eve offered her plate to Kate, saying, "Ninished, Mommy," Grace would invariably say, "I'll have it, Eve."

After one of their friend's birthday parties, I went to Grace in the middle of the night because she was crying in her sleep.

"Wake up, sweetheart, Daddy's here. You're fine. You were having a bad dream," I said, rubbing her back.

Grace put both her arms around my neck and sobbed, "I want lots of cake!" before drifting back off to sleep.

Loving and affectionate, they had the most delightful natures. One of my happiest memories is when I had finished their bedtime stories one night. Looking and sounding serious, they looked at me and then said in unison, "Daddy, we want to tell you a secret."

This was followed by each of them taking one of my ears and whispering, "We love you, Daddy."

I had been constantly saddened by the awareness that my work commitments meant that I was missing seeing them grow up. So although I was nervous about this Kindi Gym trip, I was secretly delighted that I was going to experience a bit of their world. The brutal fact was that I didn't even know where Kindi Gym was, and they had been going there for over a year.

It turned out Kindi Gym was housed in an old warehouse a short drive from Bronte. Not much gym goes on there. It's basically an enormous room packed with soft toys and apparatuses. The combination gave the place a slightly surreal feel. Among the serious gym equipment of trampolines, balance beams, pommel horses, and rings, there was a riot of brightly colored plastic slides, huge bouncing balls, crawling tunnels, and climbing frames. The floor was covered wall to wall with three layers of blue foam mats. What looked to me like a hundred kids under five were swarming noisily over everything.

I couldn't help thinking of the monkey enclosure at the zoo. Trouble was, unlike the zoo there was no viewing area for humans. Here the parents were in with the chimps—and there wasn't a latte machine or newspaper stand in sight. It seemed like hell on earth to me, but to Grace and Eve it was clearly heaven. Immediately upon being unleashed they ran off giggling and determinedly proceeded to climb up—and then fall off—each piece of equipment in turn. The padding did its job, though, and they were obviously having a whale of a time so I retreated to the side to watch. I had been told there was no structure or guided activity for the first hour to allow the children to indulge in "free-form aerobicizing." After this, one of the instructors led the children in a couple of dances to end the session.

While watching from the sidelines, I couldn't help ruminating on the mix of parents present: Apart from me, they were all mothers. Hardly surprising, I know, given that most men have to work on a weekday morning, but it suddenly seemed to be such a dramatic demarcation of roles, like some Polynesian island or Shaker community where all the men live in one hut and the women in another. If I wasn't preparing to take a year off, I would never have known this place existed, let alone be sitting in it. I suppose many boardrooms look the same in reverse—a bunch of men in a room with a solitary woman (if coffee is required). I haven't a clue how to make things more balanced, but it struck me that we've got a long way to go before roles are genuinely shared.

While indulging in this amateur sociological observation, I couldn't help noticing in an entirely unreconstructed manner that the Kindi Gym teacher was actually a real fox. Not a spare ounce of fat on her, lovely smile, brilliant with all the kids, and decked out in the type of sportswear that showed off her toned gymnast's body to dazzling effect.

In fact, was it my imagination or was she paying me special attention? She returned my smile with what I thought was very encouraging prolonged eye contact. Perhaps it was because I was the only man in the entire building. Whatever the reason, I was beginning to quite enjoy Kindi Gym.

After an hour there were three loud claps and "dance time" was announced. All the children hurriedly made their way to the end of the hall. On my way to join them, the instructor fell in besides me.

"Hi, so you're the dad of the Marsh twins?" she said.

"Yep—they seem to love it here," I replied.

"Oh they do, they never want to leave at the end."

"It's nice to see them having such a good time."

"Well, I do hope we see you here again." This was said with just a faint twinkle in her eye. I may be fat, forty, and fired, I thought, but I've obviously still got some of the old Marsh magic left.

She bounced off into the middle of the melee of children, picked up the tape recorder, and asked, "Right, kids, who wants to pick the first song to dance to?"

Grace's hand immediately tugged at the instructor's arm.

"Yes, Grace, which song shall we have today?"

The assembled crowd of kids, moms, and instructors all looked at Grace.

I looked on, positively bursting with pride.

"We don't touch Daddy's willy because it's dirty," Grace announced.

My buttocks clenched in gut-churning humiliation as thirty pairs of eyes pointedly swung my way.

"Er, it's what I say to stop them putting their hands down the toilet when I'm sitting on it." *Oh shit, this is hell,* I thought. *You're just making things worse trying to explain, you idiot. She didn't fancy you in the first place and now she's probably going to turn you in to the police.*

While driving home I consoled myself with the thought that it wasn't the worst thing one of my children had ever said. That honor was reserved for Alex, from a trip to Devon to see Granny Vi—my mother's mother—four years earlier. My mom was an only child and as such had an enormously close bond with her mother. Granny Vi had had another fall and was in intensive care in the North Devon Infirmary. The doctor's message was unequivocal—she was dying and wouldn't make it to the end of the week. She wanted to see her only great-grandson one last time. I drove through the night from London to Somerset to pick up Mom, then continued on to the hospital in Devon.

Granny Vi looked truly awful—shrunken, white, gray around the eyes. The phrase "at death's door" seemed horribly appropriate. But her eyes brightened when she saw Alex.

"Look, Mommy, Alex and Nigel have come to see you," my mom said. "And Alex has done you a picture."

"Oh that's nice, dear," Granny Vi croaked, looking at the random bunch of squiggles Alex had handed her. "What is it?"

"It's the pit of death, Granny," he sweetly replied.

Come to think of it, having the foxy gym instructor think I have a filthy knob was hardly worth worrying about.

Chapter 6

Missing the Bus

As THE LAST WEEK of my job approached, I started to get cold feet about the whole leaving work and taking a year off thing. I still hadn't made my mind up. When it came to the crunch, would I actually go through with it and not look for alternative employment?

There were a number of factors that were wobbling my resolve. The first was the fact that the firm was being incredibly reasonable and had made it clear to me that if I was prepared to be flexible about role and location there were a couple of seats still left on that bus. Second was the fact that it was worryingly clear that whenever I had attempted to sample the "good life" I was hoping a year off would give me, it had ended in unmitigated disaster.

Perhaps it wouldn't be such fun after all. Perhaps I would be bored and depressed once the initial thrill of embarking on a new adventure had waned. What would happen to my self-esteem without a job title or career to fall back on? How would other people react to me? Would I miss the stimulation and affirmation I got from the workplace? What would we actually do when the money ran out? How would Kate cope with having me around the house all day?

The third was the fact that Kate had also put a very real element of doubt in my mind. Her theory was that throughout my life and our marriage I had been a serial spurner of what was expected of me. As she put it, "You always do the opposite of what people recommend—to prove some point. Trouble is, Nigel, no one—including yourself—actually understands what that point is, or if they did understand, no one would care about it."

I suspected she was largely right. I did tend to react against situations when I felt I was being told to do what everyone else would do in the same situation. My family, in-laws, friends, work colleagues, and of course Hank had all been telling me to do nothing rash and continue collecting a paycheck. Was I just doing the opposite for the hell of it? For what it would look like? Because it would fulfill some laughable need I had to feel I was a rebel? It didn't seem particularly good reasoning upon which to base taking such a life-changing—and potentially life-ruining—step.

Having thrashed these thoughts and worries around for a couple of days, I realized I'd never know if this was the right thing to do or not unless I did it. I would have to take the leap to find out. Most workingmen who wondered if they should try stepping out of the rat race were caught in a classic catch-22 situation. They'd never know unless they did it if it was the right thing to do, but by the time they could afford to do it their kids had left home and it was too late. It was a sort of enforced inertia that kept men in a tie and at the office.

Then again, a number of men I knew used this as an excuse. They had far more money than I would ever have but they kept on raising the bar of what they needed before they would eventually feel comfortable enough to try a change. I'd had a number of conversations over the years with one particular colleague who had two houses, a share in a light aircraft, and a wife who worked. He passionately maintained he was going to take a year off "when he had enough money." He still hasn't done it—and I doubt he ever will.

I felt I had a once-in-a-lifetime opportunity to break the vicious cycle in my own life. If I knew I could feed the family for a year and I still wasn't going to do it, then I really had been emasculated. There would never be a better time. If I didn't do it now then in all honesty I was kidding myself and I would never do it. I didn't want to look back years later and say I wish I had had more courage.

In the end it was a picture I found while clearing out the boxes from my office that made my mind up. It was an archive photo of the firm's original employees in New York. It was dated 1903. It had obviously been taken at some sort of official conference. There were no women in the picture, just sixty or so men, all dressed formally with jackets and ties, sitting neatly in rows on wooden chairs in what looked like the atrium of a large office building.

I couldn't help wondering about the content of that conference. Did they talk excitedly about their plans for the company? How they were going to win new clients, expand into different markets, build offices in countries around the world? They would all be dead by now. I wondered if any of them had had any regrets at the end of their lives. If I could talk to them now, what would they say from the grave about the real value of their and the firm's achievements? What would be their definition of what was actually important? Would it be market share, double-digit growth, and shareholder value, or might their list include such things as meaningful relationships, social connectedness, and making a useful contribution? I'd never know about them, but I wanted to find out about myself.

There are no guarantees in life. Fear of the uncertain can, and does, hold millions back from pursuing their dreams. I'm not saying I wasn't scared—I was—just that I didn't want the fear to stop me. I determined I was going to look back at the end of my life and know that at least I had tried a different path—however disastrously it turned out. This year the bus would have to continue its journey with an empty seat on it.

Chapter 7

2,800 Strokes

THE FIRST DAY OF MY freedom didn't feel particularly momentous. In fact it felt like any other day. Truth was, we hadn't done any planning for our new life. It was a bit like having your first child, where you spend all the time worrying about the birth and none preparing for the next twenty years of being a parent. I had spent all my time either agonizing about whether to leave the workplace or constructing entirely unrealistic blue-sky dreams about all the earth-shattering achievements I would rattle off once I'd left the world of office work behind. No time at all had gone into thinking about how we were going to live day to day. We hadn't even discussed how we were going to divide the household chores and childcare, let alone reached any agreements.

Kate, however, was under no illusions that her life would be getting any easier. She was well aware that she was trading a qualified nanny for a useless one. To her enormous credit she didn't immediately load me up with domestic tasks to fill the hours I wasn't spending in the office. I will be forever grateful for the space and support she gave me in my often-ludicrous attempts to better myself and build a new life.

As the reality of my situation set in I began to look around for a tangible goal to focus on—over and above being a better father and husband. I've a characteristic (my wife calls it a weakness, I call it a strength, so here I'll just call it a characteristic) that once I say I'll do something I invariably do it. Be it giving up smoking (June 25, 1995, thank you very much) or doing the Sydney Harbor Bridge Run (in a breathtaking one hour and twenty minutes—the winner did it in twenty-nine minutes), once I focus on something I get an enormous pleasure out of doggedly and systematically following it through to completion. Importantly, I have also found that having a specific purpose gives me a sense of purpose generally. I'm all around a nicer and more effective person if I'm working toward something.

The last time I left a job, I decided to do, and did, the coast-to-coast walk across the north of England. This time, after a week's investigation, I decided I would do the Bondi to Bronte Ocean Swim. We lived in Bronte, one of those inner-city beach suburbs that only Sydney has, where Kate was training to be a surf life-saver. I was already learning to surf at Bondi, the beach two miles north of Bronte. The next event was in December—a suitably distant date given my total unpreparedness for such a feat.

Swimming between the two oldest surf-lifesaving clubs in the world in the third-ever Bondi to Bronte race suddenly gripped me as the perfect challenge with which to throw myself into a different lifestyle and the community. Training in the Pacific every day would certainly be a change from sitting in the bloody office for nine hours at a stretch. Besides, ocean swimming was one of the few physical activities the surgeon said I could safely do while I was healing. Apparently seawater does wonders for deep flesh wounds.

The reality of the challenge was, however, mildly daunting to a fat forty-year-old Englishman who couldn't even do free-style (the stroke in which you do the race). By all accounts swimming in the rough ocean was entirely different and much more difficult than pool swimming. When I asked one of Kate's ocean-swimming friends from the surf club what the difference was between competitive pool swimming and ocean swimming, she had snorted derisively and said, "Bluebottle jellyfish, riptides, shore dumps, seasickness." I had thought she was joking about the last one until another friend confirmed that it is apparently not uncommon for people to vomit on the longer ocean swims. Lovely.

So not only would I have to learn to swim freestyle (or front crawl, as it's called where I grew up) and get fit, I'd also have to learn the particular skill of ocean swimming. On top of it all there was also the small matter of sharks. The day of my decision, Bondi beach was closed for three hours because of a shark sighting. When the lifeguards couldn't find the beast, they reopened the beach. And here's the thing—*all the locals simply got back in the water.* Clearly I was going to need a new attitude about our finned friends, because ever since I saw *Jaws* when I was ten I'd never been truly relaxed in the sea. I was forever hearing that bloody *dur dum dur dum* music from the film in my mind.

But a goal is a goal, so I started preparations immediately.

The very next morning I walked down to the Bronte beach pool. This is one of the most remarkable features of living in this part of the world. Many of Sydney's beaches have beautiful but rugged seawater pools cut into the rocks. Unbelievably to someone who spent fifteen years living in London, these are all immaculately clean and completely free of charge. The experience of a morning swim in one of the Bondi, Bronte, Clovelly, or Coogee beach pools, while the sun rises over the horizon and the waves crash against the poolside, is simply breathtaking.

Unfortunately on this day it was slightly more breathtaking than usual. The tide was in and the sea was high. Huge rollers were breaking over the rocks and dumping into the pool, making it an enormous frothy whirlpool of water. The locals were wisely sitting this one out. Urban legend had it that the year before, a swimmer had been washed out of the pool and out to sea in particularly bad weather, and that the year before a shark had been washed *into* the pool, to the amazement of both the beast itself and the two elderly brothers who were swimming at the time.

But having made up my mind to start today, I was determined at the very least to get in the pool. Immediately upon doing so, a friendly voice yelled, "Watch out, mate." I turned in time to see a wall of green above me. Instinctively I dived to the bottom of the pool. It was like being in a giant dishwasher. The wave was the biggest one I have ever seen and it buffeted me upside down into the cliff wall with frightening force. In a perverse way, it was actually fun of sorts, but hardly appropriate practice. A change of venue was obviously in order. I got out and walked back up the hill home. I flicked through the Yellow Pages' Fitness Center section, found the number for the Hakoah Club in Bondi, and booked a swimming lesson for the next day.

Now, I've been in Irish pubs in Amsterdam, blues clubs in Tokyo, and English army bases in Cyprus, but never in all my life have I seen such a pure cultural transportation as the Hakoah Club in Bondi. You walk in and you are in Israel. I spent twelve months living in Israel, and the Wailing Wall is less like Jerusalem than the Hakoah Club.

Everyone at the Hakoah Club was delightful and friendly but for the first couple of times I visited, I did find myself turning around to look out the front door to check that my mind wasn't playing tricks on me and that I had indeed just walked off a crowded sunny street full of surfers wearing baggy shorts and straight into the Golan Heights. The ground floor itself was packed with old grannies playing the slot machines. The elevators were covered in posters that looked like they were designed in the '70s, advertising cut-price rates for the Neil Diamond impersonator night. However, upon alighting at the third floor, another cultural juxtaposition awaited. I walked into a high-tech, modern gym and pool complex and met my coach for the session—Zane.

Zane had the stomach definition of Brad Pitt in the bed-jumping scene in *Thelma and Louise,* the physical magnetism of Sean Connery in *Doctor No,* and the easygoing charm of Cary Grant at his peak. Maddeningly, on top of all these natural blessings, he was genuinely friendly, keen to help, and entirely unaware of how intimidatingly perfect he was.

I didn't feel worthy to get in the same pool as him. But then again, I wasn't entirely comfortable standing on the edge of the pool, either. I've always thought the male form is a rather pathetic sight unless it is in perfect condition (à la Zane). Dress it in a skimpy Speedo and top the whole effect off with a white paunch, swimming cap, and a pair of goggles, and it gets downright offensive. Getting in the pool seemed the better option.

I motioned to Zane that I was ready to begin.

"Excellent. Before we start, tell me, do you want to learn tumble turns, bilateral breathing, or just some simple stroke correction?" Zane asked.

"Er—it's slightly more basic than that," I replied. "I'd like you to teach me front crawl."

"You mean freestyle?"

"I think so—you know, overarm."

"Okay, dive in and show me what you can do."

I feel I should explain that in England no one does freestyle—unless they are in proper training. Because of the weather, recreational swimming is such a rare thing that the natural default stroke of almost everyone is the breaststroke. When freestyle is attempted it is only for short, one-breath-per-stroke bursts and then the universal method is to thrash your arms as fast as possible—the bigger the splash the better. The notion of controlling the stroke or using your legs is yet to catch on.

I took a deep breath and dived in. The pool was overly warm and murky. I could see hairs, Band-Aids, and broken goggles floating around on the tiles at the bottom of the pool. It felt like I was immersed in a large bowl of pubic soup.

Quickly banishing this unpleasant thought, I threw my left arm over my head then immediately followed it with my right. I wasn't sure if my forward motion was because of the dive or the strokes. I threw my left arm over my head again. I could swear I was slowly sinking. This was less swimming and more drowning with attitude. I threw my right arm past my ear and attempted a leg kick at the same time. *Now you're showing off, Nigel,* I thought to myself.

I was running out of breath but I was damned if I was going to give in. Again I threw my left arm forward, hitting the water with a rather satisfyingly large splash. Summoning all my reserves, I decided to go for another stroke—it was, after all, my first lesson and I was keen to make a good impression. As my right arm hit the water I jerked my head out of the pool and gulped four quick gasps of air. I was completely fried but actually quite pleased with myself. I'd given it my best and in the process managed to swim a full half-length of the pool. Bondi to Bronte, here I come. I could almost hear Ian Thorpe crapping himself at the prospect of me bursting on to the swimming scene.

Zane was the model of tact.

"Okay, we have some areas we could work on. But first, before we do, did you say you were intending to do the Bondi to Bronte swim?"

"Yep."

"Do you know how far that is?"

"Nope."

"Thirty-two hundred yards—two miles."

"So?"

"Well, Nigel—do you mind if I call you Nigel?—this pool is eighteen yards long. You can do half a length. That's approximately nine yards, or six strokes in your case. A good ocean swimmer would do upward of twenty-eight hundred strokes to make it from Bondi to Bronte on a calm day."

"What exactly is your point?" I said with as much false bravado as I could muster.

Chapter 8

Lower Paddock

THE START OF FEBRUARY 2003 was an extremely important time in my life. My first month out of the rat race for twenty years meant so much to me, in fact, that I ripped that page out of our family calendar and had it professionally framed and hung above my desk in the front room. Every morning when I doubted myself or thought up another excuse not to train for the Bondi to Bronte swim or thought about calling the headhunters I'd so rashly ignored, it would be a tangible reminder of the aspirations for the future I had had at the time of my decision.

February, however, wouldn't be entirely clear of distractions. My parents were arriving from England at the end of the first week to stay for a month. During their stay, Alex would have his eighth birthday and four-year-old Harry would have his first day at school. This latter rite of passage may not seem like such a big deal to some but to me it had enormous importance, rooted in my own peculiar experience of starting school.

My father was working in the Royal Navy at the time and had been posted abroad. This, and other factors to this day unexplained, led my parents to make the extraordinary decision to send me away to a boarding school in the west of England at the tender age of five.

British boarding prep schools are an invention I feel history will not judge kindly. I can't imagine the character of the Australian people or the nature of Australian society allowing such institutions to flourish here to the extent that they did over the last centuries in the United Kingdom. To my mind, a nation's prison and school systems say a lot about the country that devises them. Suffice to say, in this instance Britain obviously got the two slightly confused.

Basically these prep schools are tuition-charging schools where parents send their kids to live for three fourteen-week terms a year. The usual stay is from age seven to twelve. Just like I'm not sure it is possible for an American to understand or believe how truly idyllic Sydney is unless he comes here, similarly I don't think it is possible for an Australian to fully understand or believe the reality of what the boarding prep-school system was like in the U.K. as recently as the 1970s.

When one of the first mothers I met in Australia told me how her eight-year-old boy was "going away for ten weeks next term," my response was one of sympathy and horror. She had to explain to me that it wasn't a bad thing; it was the annual skiing trip when the entire school relocated to Thredbo Alpine Village. The kids' lessons were organized for the afternoons and evenings to enable them to ski every morning for two months. I didn't actually believe her until another friend confirmed it was true. It would be fair to say I have more affinity with a culture that sends its children on extended character-building vacations than with one that sends them to soul-destroying quasiprisons.

My memory of my arrival at prep school is as clear as if it happened yesterday. I got off the (delayed) train at Sherborne Station and, clutching my green naval-issue suitcase, presented myself to the school office. A stern-looking man with enormous eyebrows informed me I was late and that I was to put on my gym uniform and report to the Lower Paddock immediately. Matron would show me to my dormitory first.

Uttering not a single word more than "Follow me," Matron did just that and I found myself alone in a large room full of beds and wondering what my gym uniform was. I opened my suitcase to find that my mom had thoughtfully labeled its contents. To my relief, one such label had "gym uniform" on it in Mom's handwriting. Feeling slightly more confident, I put on the clothes and went in search of the Lower Paddock. When I found it, it became apparent that the whole school had received the same instructions, as 180 boys were also in their gym uniforms and were grouped in a huge semicircle facing the headmaster. Noticing me joining the group, he looked me up and down. "What's your name?" he bellowed.

"Marsh."

"Marsh Minor," he immediately corrected me. "Your brother is Marsh Major. You will be called Marsh Minor."

I didn't know what to say next. A question broke the momentary silence.

"Marsh Minor," he boomed, "what's that under your gym uniform?"

"My school uniform, sir," I replied.

"Your school uniform?"

"Yes, sir."

"You put your gym uniform on over your school uniform?"

"Yes, sir, the man told me to put on my gym uniform." Tears were welling in my eyes as it dawned on me that none of the other boys had on two pairs of shorts, four socks, or two shirts. I was only five, for Christ's sake, and no one had explained to me that you were supposed to take your uniform off before putting your gym clothes on. Not that that seemed to matter to the head-master, who was having a whale of a time publicly humiliating me.

"See this, boys, Marsh Minor obviously feels the cold! Ha ha ha, I wonder what he'll wear when we go swimming?"

This was met with an enthusiastic round of finger-pointing and jeering.

I suppose many other children had worse starts at school than me, but it was my intention that Harry wouldn't be one of them. Although Harry was going to the local public school, as opposed to a boarding prison, I was taking time off for precisely such events as his first day of school, and I would be with him, come hell or high water. The fact that my own father would be staying with me at this time somehow made it all the more important to me.

This, along with many other childhood episodes, was running through my head as I drove to the Sydney airport to pick up my parents. We hadn't seen my parents since we'd left the U.K. over a year ago, and we were all very much looking forward to seeing them again. It was a long journey for an elderly couple, and they had decided to throw some savings at business-class tickets in an attempt to minimize the trauma. I hoped they'd had a better time of it than Kate and I had on our journey out here. But then again our experience was really only traumatic because of the kids.

Our relocation to Australia was basically one catastrophe after another, started in spectacular fashion by Eve, who threw up all over the taxi driver's head before we even reached the highway leading to Heathrow. Forty embarrassing—and extremely smelly—minutes later, he pulled up outside the airport. Harry immediately asked in a loud voice, "Daddy, is this Australia? Are we there yet?"

"Not yet, sweetheart—a little while still to go," I replied, while helping Kate wipe the dried chunks of half-digested vegetables out of the poor guy's hair with the envelope of my airline ticket.

We made an imposing sight at the boarding gate, with two children, two babies, two car seats, one double stroller, and fourteen individual pieces of hand luggage (not to mention the mountain of cuddly toys and brightly colored, noisy plastic Fisher-Price detritus designed to keep babies contented that was falling out of our every pocket). The by-now well-matured aroma from Eve's performance in the taxi added nicely to the effect.

You could feel an overpowering sense of "thank Christ I'm traveling business class" from every suit-clad male in the line. When we turned left, not right, into the plane, it almost caused a riot. There was near hand-to-hand combat as the execs fought among themselves to present the most compelling case to the flight crew.

"I'm a platinum-card holder, damn it—I demand to be *down-graded*," one loudly insisted to a long-suffering flight attendant. Once order was restored, the unfortunates who had to share the business-class cabin with the family from hell settled into a groove of simmering resentment and pointedly complained every time a teddy was thrown or a spoonful of yogurt was flicked. I have no idea how many of them had originally intended to leave the plane at Singapore, but the cabin was significantly emptier for the second leg of the journey. Anyway, Mom and Dad were flying by themselves, I reasoned, so although the trip was long, it couldn't have been as bad as ours.

I parked the car while Kate got a couple of airport baggage carts for the kids to sit on. We pushed them to the arrivals gate to wait excitedly for my parents. When they walked through the gate I was shocked. I say walked, but more accurately my dad shuffled. They were old. How did that happen? Last time I'd seen them they were just Mom and Dad, but now they were bordering on frail. Not that Alex and Harry noticed, of course. They simply hurled themselves—in the way that only kids can—at Granny and Granfie in undiluted delight.

"You've got fat," my father greeted me.

"Don't worry, Dad, I'm going to lose it. How was the flight?" I replied.

"Bloody awful, a family was being relocated and they were flying business class . . ."

Chapter 9

Fat

MY DAD'S GREETING may have been untraditional and a tad insensitive, but at least it was factual—I had gotten fat. Not slightly overweight, but good, old-fashioned "if I were a woman people would think I was pregnant, pants having to be done up under the paunch, you need a heavy hammer to drive a long nail" fat. One hundred and ninety-five pounds at my last weigh-in. All my belts were on the first hole and half my shirts would no longer stretch over my belly.

In deciding to do the Bondi to Bronte race, I'd vaguely acknowledged that I might need to shed the odd pound, but now I realized I had to get serious. I added yet another resolution for my year off: Once and for all, I would sort out my size. Not in an unsustainable, one-time way like those wonderfully pointless "lose weight for the summer and look great in your bikini" diets that women's magazines promote every year. It has always struck me as absurd that people would want to starve themselves for months to look good in their swimsuit for a few weeks and then go back to looking like a sack of crap for the rest of the year. I wanted a permanent, livable-with change, something that would sort it for good and therefore free me from ever having to think, or worse, talk about it again.

I had consulted various books and one of those machines you see in drugstores that tell you not just your weight but what you should weigh. Taking a balanced view, I was at least thirty-five pounds overweight. I decided to set myself a goal of losing two pounds a week until I was under 155 pounds and then remaining under 155 pounds until, and beyond, the Bondi to Bronte swim in December. If I stuck to the two-pounds-a-week schedule, I would be under 155 pounds by July and then have six months to learn how to stay at that weight before the race. My strategy to lose the fat was a simple one: Eat less and exercise more. I was relying on willpower for the former and training for the swim for the latter.

I've read a lot of advice in my time about diets and weight loss, and almost without exception it has all been nonsense. It seemed to me that because it was such a simple issue, people couldn't bear having the stark reality of it played back at them, so they willingly went along with all sorts of bullshit that enabled them to ignore the bald truth: They were overweight because they ate too much and exercised too little. I had long wanted to write a diet book, provisionally entitled *Stop Moaning and Eat Less, You Fat Bastard,* and now seemed a perfect time to test my theory out on myself. If it worked, I seriously intended to write the book—although perhaps with a more sensitive title.

As we waited at the baggage carousel for Mom and Dad's bags, I couldn't help noticing all the overweight people in the crowds around us. I wondered how many of them were unhappy with their body image or were permanently on a variety of ineffectual diets, one after the other. It struck me as a sad and entirely avoidable state of affairs. Life is full of uncertainties. There are no agreed rules on how to be happy or rich or spiritually rewarded. Half the time we work determinedly toward a goal not really knowing whether what we are doing is the right way to get us there. It has always seemed to me that weight loss is the rare exception. Everyone knows what to do. No one disagrees. The issue is totally within each individual's control. It isn't that people don't know what to do, it's just that they are, by and large, incapable of doing it.

The whole weight-loss industry was focused in the wrong direction. New methods of eating differently weren't what was required. In my opinion, what was needed was advice on how to maintain the motivation to sustain the behavior that would lead to weight loss. Basically, in an increasingly spoiled and soft society, people had lost the ability to delay gratification for any prolonged period of time. The moment they felt hungry or sad or in need of a reward or whatever, their willpower crumbled and they behaved in a way they knew was contradictory to their own desire to be thin.

To avoid the feeling of shame that comes with living with this self-knowledge, they all conspired with the writers, who gave them the face-saving out of the latest new science or theory about how to lose weight. No one, it seemed, was prepared to stand up and state the truth in a compelling way—if you are fat it's usually because you eat too much.

I, Nigel Marsh, was going to single-handedly transform my own body and then write a best-seller that would forever change the diet industry and help countless millions around the world fulfill their dreams in a way they had never been able to before. With that inspirational thought, I pushed the baggage cart into the airport McDonald's and bought the kids a Happy Meal each with extra large fries and a Quarter Pounder with Cheese for myself.

Chapter 10

Applecatchers

My parents had planned their trip months before. Obviously none of us knew then that I would be unemployed and hanging around the house during their visit. Their presence had advantages and disadvantages in equal measure. It was great to see them, but the fact that both of them thought I was insane to have left work added to the stress of an already weird situation. Kate and I hadn't quite come to grips with it ourselves yet.

We had a lot of adjusting to do. First up we had to let our delightful nanny, Charmaine, go. This was sad to do—the kids adored her—but we just wouldn't be able to afford her help over the coming months. The day after we told the kids she was leaving, Grace took my hand, led me to the map of the world stuck to her bedroom wall, pointed at it sadly, and asked, "Daddy, where is Nannyworld?"

"'Nannyworld,' sweetheart?" I said.

"Nannyworld, where Liz, Shannon, Emma, Terry, and Laura live?" she trustingly explained.

"Oh, it's here," I said, pointing vaguely at Canada, all the time wondering if this was going to irreversibly mess her up when she found out there was no such place as Nannyworld. I found it so difficult to know when to play along and when to be factual and accurate. I had visions of her being laughed at in the playground as she insisted to a bunch of geographically wise classmates that Canada was actually Nannyworld.

Perhaps my worries were so acute because of my own similar childhood blunders. I still blush now, thirty-five years later, when remembering the time at school that I got into a fight with a class-mate because he didn't believe me when I said Pete Townsend lived in the north of England in Leeds. A crowd of older boys broke up the fight and then ended up getting involved in the debate themselves. Given my passionate insistence that I *knew* where Pete Townsend lived, I was given the chance to present some evidence to prove my case. Eagerly I rushed off to my older brother's dormitory and moments later returned triumphantly with his copy of the live concert album *The Who Live in Leeds*. Maybe I should have cleared up the whole Nannyworld/Canada thing with Grace after all.

We'd been blessed with the people we'd managed to convince over the years to help us with the demands of four kids and a useless absentee father. It was going to be strange having no one else around in the family, because ever since the twins were born we'd always had someone to help, even if it was only for a few hours a week. It would, I supposed, be nice to have the house totally to ourselves once more. It does rather limit the naked bedroom-to-bathroom walking, shouting arguments, and sitting-room sex when you've got a twenty-two-year-old student liable to walk in at any time.

Then again, it wasn't just the family who had to put up with the nanny—the nanny also had to put up with the family. On the second morning of my parents' visit I was in the kitchen while the rest of the family was having breakfast. I wanted to go for a swim and was looking through an overflowing laundry basket for a towel when I came across an enormous pair of underpants.

"Jesus, darling, if you're going to have an affair you might at least have the decency to hide his underwear from me," I said to Kate.

"Never seen them before—blimey, they are enormous. Perhaps they're your dad's?" she replied.

"Nope, not mine," said my dad, who had just walked in. "In the navy we used to call those applecatchers."

Laughing, my mom joined in: "Granny Knickers is what we used to call circus tents like those."

I stretched them above my head. "We could make a shade in the garden out of them—if you're sure your lover won't miss them," I said to Kate.

"He wouldn't, but I might," a visibly upset Charmaine whispered as she grabbed them out of my hands and walked up the stairs.

"Damn it, Kate, why didn't you tell me they were hers?" I demanded.

"I told you, I'd never seen them before," she replied.

Perhaps a break from Nannyworld wasn't such a bad idea after all.

Chapter 11

Venus

AT THE SAME TIME that we were getting rid of things from our life—asking nannies to leave, selling cars, and looking for cheaper houses to move to—I was also trying to add things. For a start I wanted to agree on a swimming schedule with Kate. It was all well and good deciding I was going to train for the race, but with four young kids, and now no nanny, this would inevitably be an extra burden on Kate. On top of the swimming schedule I also wanted to sign up to do things that would force me to engage in the community and experience a different side of life. School cafeteria duty was the main thing I had in mind at this early stage.

But it wasn't just life outside the office that I wanted to experience—I was after an overall less-male existence. Ever since being sent to a single-sex boarding school at the age of five, I felt I had led a particularly male-dominated life. Frankly, women were a mystery to me. They seemed to live in a different world. I had read *Men Are from Mars, Women Are from Venus* a couple of years back and, leaving aside the easy criticisms that can be made of it, I had found it a powerful eye-opener. Some of women's behavior was so damn strange.

One of my earliest memories of living with Kate is of her coming home from the office we both worked at exclaiming, "I'm dying to go to the bathroom."

"Why didn't you go before you left?" I asked.

"I couldn't. There was someone in there," she replied.

"You've only got one stall in the ladies' room at work?" I asked.

"No, about six."

"And they were all in use? Wow, rush hour down at the old powder room," I commented.

"They weren't all engaged. One of them was," Kate said.

"But you said there are six stalls in there," I queried.

"There are, but I can't go if someone else is in the room," she explained.

"Why the hell not?"

"Because they might hear."

"Hear what?"

"Me going to the bathroom."

"But it's a toilet, for Christ's sake."

"You don't understand. I could never take a poop if someone else was in the room."

"Bloody hell! In the men's we have conversations with each other over the walls," I told her.

"That's revolting! While you're going to the toilet?" she asked.

"Yep. Some guys even take their phones in and carry on working."

"None of my friends would ever do that."

"You mean it's not just you? Other women think like this as well?" I said.

"Absolutely."

Clearly a different world—and one I was keen to learn more about as the year progressed. To do so would require not just a change in mind-set and some proper empathetic listening, it would also require that I be disciplined in how I spent my time. Already it was clear to me that it would be possible to kid myself and spend the year doing the glory bits of parenting—the high-attention, high-reward, interactive, fun bits like taking the kids out, doing the school run, and going to sporting events with them. While these were all valuable, I was aware that they were only the tip of the iceberg. Perverse as it may sound, I actually wanted to do the drudgery bits as well—the cooking, cleaning, and shopping stuff. I don't want to attempt to portray myself as a saint—something tells me it would be less than convincing if I did—but it is fair to say I was genuine in my desire to look beyond my one-dimensional male world and be slightly less useless as a partner.

When I mentioned these high ideals to Kate, she naturally had a different perspective. "I believe you, Nigel. No, no, I do. I'm sure if you get huge amounts of praise and attention for doing so you'll lend your hand to the drudgery."

I may not have understood her world, but she was clearly fluent in mine.

Chapter 12

Muffia

WHILE MY MOM AND DAD stayed with us, Kate and I agreed that it would be reasonable for me to plan on training for the swim three times a week. We also signed me up to do cafeteria duty at Alex's school. Truth is, I've always been a bit of a goal junkie and already the list of goals was becoming quite daunting. I wanted to be a better father and a better husband, train for an ocean swim, lose thirty pounds, get involved in the community, and attempt to get in touch with my feminine side—or at least a more feminine point of view. All of them, to my mind, were worthwhile goals but it didn't really have the look of a very relaxing existence.

At least the swimming was easy to organize. On a good day I could stroll down the hill, have a swim in the Bronte ocean pool, and be back to wake Kate up with a cup of tea before the kids stirred. But while it may have been easy to organize, I was finding it less easy to *do*. Zane had given me a load of good advice but the simple fact of the matter was I found freestyle awkward and exhausting. After a couple of weeks I was still incapable of doing it for anything but the shortest of times. At the end of February, on the morning of Alex's eighth birthday, I managed three lengths and was pathetically delighted with myself. Then again, it *was* an improvement. I've always been a believer in the philosophy that if you are moving consistently in the right direction it doesn't ultimately matter how slowly you are going. Twenty-five more years like this and I'd be able to swim the Tasman Sea.

Rather encouragingly, I had stopped putting on weight. The bathroom scales even indicated a minor improvement. I still looked like the Michelin Man with my clothes off, but I felt it was the start I needed.

Parenting-wise I was trying my best but overambition, lack of practice, and general ignorance was my undoing. For Alex's party I thought it would be a good idea to have sixteen eight-year-olds stay for a sleepover. The only place I could fit them all was on the floor of the hallway in sleeping bags. Turns out it was a good idea—way too much of a good idea. They were so excited I couldn't shut the little buggers up. The more excited they got, the louder they became and the worse they behaved. The worse they behaved, the louder I shouted. I felt like that one lousy teacher we all knew who couldn't control the children in his lessons. For some reason everyone always pissed around in his class no matter what he did or threatened, while the other teachers could keep perfect control without raising their voices once. I clearly was going to need to learn a different strategy than shouting.

Fortunately, Harry's first day at school went better than Alex's party, and gloriously all my worries proved to be mere projections from my own experience. Granfie, Alex, Harry, and I walked to school on the first morning. Harry chatted happily the whole way. Dad and I walked on either side of him, held a hand each, and swung him in the air every five steps. When we got to the school gates he ran in to meet his classmates without a backward glance. I, on the other hand, was sick with worry all day, imagining all sorts of bullying and mental torment, but at pick-up time he was the same picture of contentment. In fact, Dad and I both had to hang around for an age while he played "kick cricket" with a tennis ball with his brother and the older boys. (Australians' love of sport doesn't let a simple fact like lack of the proper equipment get in the way of a game.) We walked home via the newsstand so we could treat them both to an ice cream.

My first school cafeteria day was also a success. I had been a bit worried going into it as the day before, a still-working mate of mine spent the whole evening in the pub telling me what a vicious environment schools were.

"It makes office politics seem like a picnic," was his opening gambit.

"What does?" I replied.

"The playground."

"Yeah, kids can be awful, I know," I agreed.

"No, not the kids, the kids are fine. It's the parents who are the nightmare."

"You're joking."

"Deadly serious, brother. There's a pecking order every bit as complex and mean-spirited as at the office."

"It can't be that bad."

"Look, once you've been snubbed by the Muffia you'll never forget it."

"What the hell's the Muffia?" I asked.

"The handful of moms you get in every school who run things."

"You mean the heads of the various committees and the like?"

"No, not necessarily. The Muffia don't literally run things, they really run things."

"Oh, I see," I said, still confused.

"They are the real influencers who work everything out behind the scenes through a hidden unofficial network. Get on the wrong side of them and you're totally screwed. They don't take prisoners," he said.

Luckily I had a gentle landing as I either didn't meet the Muffia or they were undercover and being nice to me on my first day. The moms I shared cafeteria duty with were delightful, friendly, and helpful. Making and doling out 250 cafeteria lunches was enormously satisfying and fun. It was also a real thrill seeing the look of pleasure in both my sons' eyes when they saw me behind the counter from the lunch line.

"Hey look, that's my dad. He sucks at surfing. He keeps falling off," Harry said, nudging the boy in front of him.

Alex had a more direct but equally random and damning angle.

"Hi, Dad, ham pizza. In Indonesia, rather than using the word 'very' before a word they just repeat the word. Banana milk, please. So you would be 'fat fat' not 'very fat.' Cool, isn't it? And a cheese stick. Thanks."

Rather than feel deflated, I felt blessed to have seen and experienced a little bit of their world. I was keen keen, as they say in Indonesia, to go back.

Chapter 13

Lip and Chin

MY NEW LIFE wasn't just packed with self-imposed goals, it was also full of surprises—and learning. For a start, where did all the people come from? I had always imagined when I was in the office that town centers would be empty. But they weren't. They were teeming with people—women and men. Didn't they have jobs to go to? Evidently the entire population didn't spend from nine to five in an office building.

I also began to understand why women were so damn rude when you called them in the late afternoons. It had always irritated me at the end of a hard working day when I would call Kate up for a chat and get short shrift from her.

"Hi, sweetheart, it's me," I would usually start.

"Yes. What do you want?" she would invariably reply.

"Nothing, just a chat."

"I can't, I'm busy."

"Busy? Doing what?"

"Looking after your sodding children."

"Well, if you can't talk, could you put Alex on?"

"No."

"Why not?" I'd ask.

"He's in the bath."

"Harry then?"

"Nigel, I haven't got time for this. They are all in the bath."

"Jesus, sorry I called," I would mutter as I hung up.

Thing is, after only a month off I now knew how incredibly irritating it was if anyone called you during the bath-time and bedtime hour that made up the end of each day. It is called arsenic hour, and for good reason. You are tired, the kids are getting cranky, and you have an amazing amount of stuff to do in a very short space of time. All it takes is a daughter being difficult during her hair washing or a husband who wants to chat on the phone and the whole delicate system collapses and no one gets to bed until ten o'clock. As any mother knows, this is an absolute disaster because it means that the whole day is given over to childcare with no space left for you to be an independent adult before your own bedtime.

Now that I wasn't working, I had never spent more time together with Kate. We would actually meet *during* the day, a welcome development after ten years of living separate lives on weekdays. Previously we had worked hard in different areas toward different ends—her raising the kids, me building a career. Now, for the first time in our marriage, we were engaged in shared endeavors toward one common end—living successfully together as a family. This was not as easy as it may sound, and it also wasn't always fun. In fact, I found certain aspects of my new life maddening—in particular the way Kate reacted to my efforts to help around the house.

This was entirely new ground for me, as previously with our separate roles it was accepted that the household and child-rearing chores fell to Kate. So not only did I now have to conquer my natural laziness but also my extensive ignorance. I constantly found I didn't know what to do in the simplest of situations. It was one thing being asked to "dress the girls," but it was quite another knowing what they should wear and where those clothes actually were. Kate didn't exactly help with me with the transition.

"Oh no, not in that!" she exclaimed the first time I emerged from the girls' bedrooms with two dressed twins.

"Why not?"

"Because I never put those tops with those skirts," she replied.

"Why not?" I asked.

"I prefer it if they wear their green tops with those skirts," she explained.

"But you asked *me* to dress them," I protested.

"Yes, but I like them in a different outfit."

"Yes, but you asked me to dress them—I've dressed them. They look fine."

"No need to get upset about it—I'll quickly change them."

"No, you won't," I replied.

"Why not?" Kate asked.

"Because I want them to wear what they've got on. What I, their father, chose for them to wear. You are always doing this. You ask me to do something and when I do it, the first—the very first—thing you do is criticize. It really pisses me off. How about saying something really radical like, 'Thanks for dressing the girls, darling'?" I asked.

"Typical, men always want thanks for doing the simplest of tasks," she replied. "When do I get thanked? I dress the girls all the time and you never thank me. Why should I thank you when you do the basic things that you should be doing anyway?"

"Because I would like it, and it would encourage me in my efforts to be helpful," I told her.

"I shouldn't have to say 'thank you' to get you to do the chores," she answered.

"You know what? You're right—you shouldn't. However, I want to be clear with you. It really depresses me that doing such a simple thing as saying 'thank you' to your husband causes you such a problem. How difficult is it to say the bloody words 'thank you'? What possible harm could it do you? This shouldn't be some sort of point-scoring competition. If it makes me happy and doesn't cost you anything to do, why not do it anyway? Pretend to be grateful, for Christ's sake. What possible outcome are you after by not thanking me and making the first words out of your mouth a criticism? Just imagine for a second that you said, 'Thanks' and didn't mention that you didn't agree with my choice of clothes. Would it kill you? Or would we have a pleasant morning and the next day I would want to dress the girls again and you could suggest in advance what they should wear and I would agree and I wouldn't think you were a mean-spirited cow who needed her mustache waxed?"

"God, I hate you when you are like this," Kate replied.

Although I felt I had right on my side (men always do), my last remark was ever so slightly below the belt. Only the day before, Kate had been to the beauty salon—the delightfully named Backs, Cracks, and Sacs—for a leg waxing appointment. The lady who greeted her at the door had taken a lingering look at her face and said, "So, dear, you're in for a lip and chin?" Kate, the angel, had died on the spot, agreed, and came back home with a smooth chin and hairy legs.

Later that night, when I had calmed down, I resolved to get to the bottom of this issue—fairly. I had, after all, promised Kate that if I took time off work I would try to be less of an asshole. Our conversation was a real education. When she explained it to me—and I was properly listening as opposed to trying to beat her in an argument—I could actually see her point. More than that, I actually found myself agreeing with her.

Turns out she wasn't being a mean-spirited bitch—and she hasn't got a mustache either—it's just that she comes at it from a completely different perspective. To her, to have to thank me for doing basic tasks is demeaning. It makes her feel servile, like she is in an inferior role to me. It makes her feel that the childcare is entirely her role and I'm being gracious in condescending to dip in and help her every now and then.

I could see how this would piss her off, given that I was spending all the family's savings specifically so I could spend a year off properly engaging with the family. We ended up after two bottles of wine agreeing that I would attempt to be less of a needy jerk and she would attempt to limit her criticisms to those occasions when my fashion taste was a crime against humanity, as opposed to simply poor.

Besides parenting, the other area where I wasn't progressing as quickly as I'd have liked was in my swimming training.

I had been finding it hard work and unenjoyable. I had been doing it for a month and, progress or not, it was clear I was useless at it. Then a breakthrough came, courtesy of my friend David Fleeting. David was a parent at the school and a lifeguard at Bronte beach. He swam most days in the ocean, regardless of the weather. He had also done both the previous Bondi to Bronte races and was someone whom I had taken into my confidence regarding my swimming goal. It was too embarrassing and expensive to continue with Zane, so David had taken the role of my unofficial adviser.

"How's the swimming going, Nige?" David asked one day while we were both waiting in the school playground at pick-up time.

"Shitty," I said. "I'm only up to five lengths of the Bronte pool but finding it really hard work."

"Are you doing bilateral breathing?" he asked.

"Trying," I replied.

"Using your legs?"

"Trying," I replied.

"Going fast?"

"Trying."

"Right, I want you to try this next time. Don't bother with your legs at all."

"But I'll sink," I protested.

"Don't be an idiot, of course you won't. The legs only give you ten percent of your power anyway. Forget about them for now."

"Okay. Is that it?"

"No. I also want you to forget the bilateral breathing, but most important, I want you to go as slowly as you can."

"As slowly?" I asked.

"Yep, as slowly. Don't worry what anyone else thinks, just plod along. You need to find your 'jogging' pace."

The very next morning I put his advice into practice and was stunned by the results. I did ten lengths—easily. I may still have looked like the proverbial rugby player doing ballet but I was totally delighted. Five weeks before I couldn't swim a length. It finally felt like I was getting somewhere.

Chapter 14

Walk on the Grass

WITH HARRY SAFELY in school and my swimming schedule started in earnest, I now wanted to dedicate myself to spending some quality time with my parents. Or, more accurately, getting to know my parents. If you go to boarding school when you are five years old, you effectively leave home—with all that this entails. It's a simple, if sad, fact that from the tender age of five, I spent considerably more time in the care of teachers at school than with my parents. When I was left on that first day, I didn't see my parents again for fourteen weeks.

Now, at the time I knew nothing else, so I simply got on with it. At the age of forty with four kids of my own, I find the notion utterly barbaric. I couldn't possibly send Harry away at the age he is now, or even Alex, who is three years older than I was then.

What were my parents thinking? Harry still asks me to check if his bottom is clean and if I will lie down with him after his bedtime story. At Sherborne Prep I received no love or tenderness. Ever.

My personal space amounted to a bed in a dormitory with thirty other boys, a desk in a classroom with forty other boys, and a wire mesh locker with two hooks in it in a changing room shared by 180 others. No visits, no privacy, no trips beyond the school grounds, no girls, no weekends off, no hugs, no stories, no tenderness—just the law of the jungle until the end of term. I used to look at the clock in class and every time the minute hand clicked one dash forward I would mentally cheer that I was a minute nearer going home.

On my first night at the school—after the gym uniform incident—one boy in my dorm had made the mistake of crying because he was so homesick. His anguished sobs sounded like the noise a sports car makes as it goes up though the gears. Every night after, for the next fourteen weeks, he was taunted until he cried.

"Where's Mommy? Do you think she's missing you? Who's feeding your rabbit? Bet your sister had ice cream for tea . . ."

If this didn't work, stealing his teddy bear and repeatedly stomping on its head would normally do the trick. Everyone would then lie back and laugh as he went though the gears.

But when I wrote home (we had to write a letter home every Saturday), I was at pains to say how happy I was, because I thought that was what my parents wanted to hear and I didn't want to let them down. I feel this point marked the beginning of an emotional superficiality between us. One boy did make a stab at writing the truth, but the master who read all the letters before they got sent out made him change it.

It makes my blood boil when I hear some militaristic blowhard talking about how such experiences are character building. Yeah, right, and what type of character? I know people who never recovered from prep school. I think I would be a therapist's dream. To this day I still crave appreciation, public praise, and signs of affection. I also find myself repeatedly and unexpectedly falling into bouts of loneliness and despair, strangely usually when I'm in the most jovial and loving company.

Prep school didn't just mean my school days were some sort of *Lord of the Flies* hell. It also ruined what was left of my home life. When I eventually got home after the first fourteen weeks, I had changed irreversibly. Moreover, my parents and I had no common ground. It was like the opposite of a good marriage, where you build up shared experiences. From the time I was five we were living separate lives, coming together sporadically as polite strangers who happened to be related.

Anyway, for this and many other reasons, I was determined to try to make up for lost time and genuinely connect with my mother and father before it was too late. This was not as easy as I had hoped. Then again, my strategy probably wasn't very realistic. I decided that I would ask them each out for dinner individually. I reasoned this would give me the time to talk properly to them and go beyond the usual polite chitchat without distractions. In reality, I think the invitations really spooked them. Kate told me that she felt certain that they thought I had booked the dinners to tell them something awful, as they had the look of two people bracing themselves for bad news.

Both dinners turned out to be delightful but not really what I was after. It rapidly became clear to me on the evening I took my mother out that she thought I was going to tell her over dinner that Kate and I were getting divorced. It took me until dessert to convince her that we weren't splitting up. Dad had different suspicions about what our evening together meant.

"Do you need money, Nigel?" he asked as soon as we sat down in the restaurant.

"No, I've got my credit card with me, Dad. Tonight's on me."

"No, not tonight. I mean do you need money? Are you and Kate having trouble?"

"Dad, we're fine. Relax, I just wanted to have you to myself for an evening."

"Why?" he asked.

"To chat."

"About what?"

"I don't know, anything," I replied. "Career advice?"

"Really?"

"Yeah, it's a start, why not? How did you go about managing your career?"

"Simple. I made a point of doing whatever the navy asked me. I deliberately set out to get a reputation for being a person they could call on to do the jobs no one else wanted. It didn't matter if I liked the assignment or not, I just wanted to keep my job. Any job. That way I knew I would always have a salary. That's the key thing, Nigel—stay employed. You've got to think of your responsibilities. You've a wife and four kids to look after," he said, sounding strangely like Hank.

I didn't really need another "seat on the bus" chat, so I changed the subject to more comfortable and superficial topics.

The next day Kate and I agreed that maybe a group occasion was more appropriate than the one-on-one approach. Perhaps if we could combine a family dynamic with a special event it would help prompt the intimacy I was after. Luckily, we had just such an event up our sleeves. The year before, my brother, Jon, had visited Sydney and gone to a restaurant in a national park north of the city that you access by seaplane. It's called the Cottage Point Inn, and he had raved about it so much that Mom had called up from England and told us that, as a surprise thank-you gift, she had booked us all on the same flight on the strength of Jon's recommendation.

I was delighted, not just because it was another opportunity to bond with my folks, but also because for me the Australian attitude about air travel was yet another wonderful aspect of the life here. It may make me a geek to admit it but I actually *like* the Sydney airport: Well designed, welcoming, and with lots of space, it is the precise opposite of Heathrow. The Sydney airport wasn't what I liked best, however, it was the smaller airports—and airplanes—that had grabbed me. The smaller the better.

I had come to completely revise my opinion of plane trips. When I lived in the U.K., a plane journey rarely lasted less than six hours and always involved at least a 150-seater aircraft and a visit to either of the appalling Heathrow or Gatwick airports. Since coming to Australia I had experienced a whole succession of stress-free, exciting, and short flights from airports with terminals no bigger than the average house.

Flying was simply no big deal—it was how you got around. It was no more special than train travel used to be in England; in fact there were many similarities. On one flight from Hervey Bay to Brisbane, the pilot announced, "Our flight time to Maryborough will be five minutes." I remember thinking I must have misheard him, but sure enough, five minutes later we were pulling up outside Maryborough "airport," which looked more like a village shop in *Thomas the Tank Engine*—complete with white picket fence out front—than an airport.

I started to keep a personal record of airports visited—Newcastle, Gladstone, Uluru, Hervey Bay, Bankstown, Lord Howe, Albury. Each was wonderful in its own way. My favorite to date was Jindabyne. I had been on vacation when an emergency call had come through. I had to get back to the office pronto. I couldn't take the car and leave the family stranded, so the company booked one of those short-hop flights.

When the cab dropped me off, I was convinced there had been a mistake. Not only was there no terminal or taxi stand, *there was no runway*. In fact, there was nothing beyond a handwritten sign on the gate to the field that rather grandly stated "Jindabyne Aerodrome." I searched the countryside for any other sign of air transportation. I couldn't see any of the traditional clues, not even a windsock—nothing. But I was in the right place. After a short wait, Avant Air Flight Number 2 appeared on the horizon and buzzed the field once before bumpily landing on the rutted grass and taxiing up to my side. In the U.K. taking your own four-seater plane is the behavior of an oil magnate or multimillionaire. In this case it was costing the firm considerably less than the price of a taxi from Gatwick to the center of London.

On the day Mom had booked for the flight to Cottage Point, we drove the couple of miles to Rose Bay, the site of Sydney's old water airport. I was doubly excited as I'd never flown in a seaplane before. The water airport had once thrived, but now it consisted solely of a hut the size of a phone booth on a wooden jetty jutting into the harbor opposite Shark Island.

The plane was also tiny—so small, in fact, that I had to sit in the copilot's seat, with Kate and my parents crammed in behind me. The pilot was typical of the people we had met since our arrival in Australia: cheerful, helpful, and humorous. His in-flight safety announcement was a classic.

"In the event of an emergency you'll find the emergency door located on your right," he said, pointing at the very door we had all just climbed in. There wasn't any other door. It was *the* door.

The in-flight service was equally wonderful.

"Would you care for a light refreshment?" he asked us as we taxied away from the jetty.

"Yes thanks, that would be nice," my mom replied.

"Excuse me, mate, would you mind passing me that bag?" the pilot asked me, pointing to a rucksack at my feet. I lifted the bag across my lap and gave it to him, whereupon he reached inside, took out a plastic bottle of water, opened it, and passed it to Mom. British Airways business class, eat your heart out.

He was clearly an excellent pilot, taking us on a short but breathtaking journey, swooping first over the harbor and then the national park before coming in to land on the Hawkesbury River and pulling up alongside the restaurant terrace. A four-course lunch followed that could only be described as bliss. Mom and Dad were in sparkling form and Kate looked radiant, beautiful and relaxed.

After years of trying to engineer an open and engaged relationship with my parents, here I was drinking and laughing with them while our own private plane waited to fly us home whenever we so desired. If this was what not working was like, it definitely got my vote. Then again, to be fair, not working back home in England probably wouldn't have been so idyllic. This day trip was the type of thing that you can do only in Sydney. The city is full of so many unexpected delights that Kate and I had fallen totally in love with the place.

The love affair started on our very first visit to the country, when we came to look for a house before my job started. We were walking in the Botanical Gardens behind the Opera House when we came across a sign: please do walk on the grass. I did a double take and looked closer. Sure enough, the council had erected a sign saying please do walk on the grass. Underneath, in smaller letters, the writing continued: and talk to the plants and hug the trees. it's your park, it's here for you to enjoy. have fun. I was stunned and have never really been the same since.

Barely a week has gone by in the last three years when I haven't had a "Sydney moment." Whether it's the outdoor movies, the New Year's Eve fireworks, an unexpected view of the Harbor Bridge, the ocean pools, the harbor, the beaches, or gay Mardi Gras, the city never ceases to amaze and delight me. I am utterly biased and find it impossible to imagine a nicer, happier city on the entire planet.

On their own, the harbor or the surf beaches or Centennial Park would be enough to make a city. Sydneysiders have to put up with having all three. With the stunning ocean and harbor coast within fifteen miles of the Opera House, you can't drive for more than ten minutes without falling across yet another natural wonder. Unlike London, where you feel that unless you win the lottery you'll never get a slice of the action, in Sydney "ordinary" people really can surf before work or swim at the end of the day.

While I had been working I constantly felt like I was missing out on the best that Sydney had to offer. I resolved to make the most of the city now that I had the chance. My birthday gave me another excuse to do just that. I left nothing to chance and planned it myself and, fortunately, it went perfectly according to plan.

The kids woke me up with presents (I didn't shout once), then I went for an early morning run along the Bondi to Bronte coast path before having breakfast with my parents. Then Kate and

I did the short drive to Lady Bay Beach to do our traditional birthday skinny dip (have I mentioned before that Sydney is an incredible place? It even has a nudist beach *in* the city), before lunch with pals at Watsons Bay, looking across at the bridge and Opera House.

This was followed by an afternoon of surfing at Bondi and tea with the kids at home before ending the day by going to a film in the Botanical Gardens' open-air cinema with Kate and my parents. It was *Gangs of New York*—total unmitigated rubbish despite all the fawning reviews. But by that stage of the day I was so happy I didn't care. For me it really was the perfect birthday, and it served as a fitting end to my parents' visit, for in the morning they were flying home.

But the next day, while driving back home from the airport having waved Mom and Dad off, I couldn't stop my mind from wandering to the darker side of my situation. It had only been a few weeks. Of course I was having a good time now. But what about when the initial excitement wore off? With my parents and Charmaine gone, we now had no extra help with the kids, so there would inevitably be less free time than before.

What about when the money started to run out? All my projects and goals were fine and honorable, but losing weight and doing an ocean swim wouldn't pay the bills. I had four young children, and neither my wife nor I currently had a job. We had no income whatsoever. The situation, viewed in a coolly rational way, was actually rather serious. I've always taken my family responsibilities seriously. Something had to be done. I made a decision to do something that was at least proactive—if not entirely what the situation called for. I booked a vacation for myself away from Sydney, the family, and, I hoped, my worries.

Chapter 15

Leaded Gasoline

TASMANIA IS IN MANY ways the perfect place to run away to. If I couldn't escape from my worries buried deep within a wilderness listed as a World Heritage site, at the edge of the earth, then where could I? It would be easy to paint the trip as self-indulgent. In fact it *was* self-indulgent, and enormously inconvenient for Kate. But at the same time it was only a week away, and it was precisely what I needed. I was supposed to be embarking on a new, more considered life away from work, but instead the operation and recovery process, my parents' visit, the final details of actually leaving the job, the demands of the kids, and coming to grips with the whole new world of being a proper part of running a household, plus my absurdly ambitious swimming goal, meant

I was caught up in what seemed like a constant blur of activity and noise.

I hadn't stopped and reflected properly on what I wanted—really wanted. Running around like a headless chicken, filling every waking second with activity, was not what I originally had in mind when I was lying on my stomach at Christmas dreaming of a career break. If I carried on the way I was going I might as well have stayed at work.

My first day off work had been a false start. I, or the world, hadn't changed. One day had just run into another, then another. I wanted to make this trip a watershed—the week when I sorted out some fundamentals in my mind so that when I got back home I could make a fresh start and continue the way I meant to go on. I also wanted to get drunk and walk up a few mountains with my good mate Jon.

Jon is one of my friends from college. I've known him for over twenty years. I was an usher at his wedding and he was an usher at mine. I am godfather to one of his gorgeous children and he is godfather to one of mine. By a bizarre coincidence, he had moved to Melbourne a few months after Kate and I had moved to Sydney.

Yet another of my problems with the conventional world of work for male executives is it's all too easy to neglect your nonwork mates. Between the twin demands of office and family, there just doesn't seem to be the time to keep up any significant relationships with them. For most men this is a real loss. The people I know who have managed to maintain a meaningful connection with friends outside of their work are without exception noticeably happier and more relaxed than those who haven't been able to.

There is a growing body of opinion among certain academics that "social capital" is as important a measure of genuine success as "financial capital," and the next big battle for developed economies will be to recognize and adapt to this reality. Irrespective of the truth of this theory, Jon was the friend I did the coast-to-coast walk with eight years ago, the last time I had a major career change, and now that I was embarking on another one I was delighted he was joining me again.

Apart from the fact that we get along and he is great company, he was also the perfect companion for this particular trip as he was ideally suited for enabling me to confirm my prejudices about the life choice I had made. Jon was in a different industry from the one I'd just left, but his role was every bit as high-pressured. Each day I'd goad him about how crappy his job was and then smugly listen as he poured out his woes about how out of balance his life was.

I'd use these sessions to retrospectively justify my supposedly heroic stance against the machine, when in reality Jon's woes were the normal tales of any workingman. I was grasping at straws to assuage the guilt of not having immediately jumped back on the treadmill as so many of my friends, ex-colleagues, and family members were urging. The irony of me talking about wanting a more balanced life as I gently strolled around the Apple Isle with no job or family to bother me, having left my wife alone to fend for herself with four young kids, was something I didn't dwell on.

Given my situation, we had set—and agreed to stick to—a tight budget. Frequent-flyer miles had covered my return flight, so transport within Tasmania was the next big item to take care of. We rented the cheapest car we could find from the cheapest firm we could find. No offense to Toyota, but I have never before or since been in a worse vehicle than the hundred-year-old Corolla we were presented with at the airport. The Crapolla, as we affectionately dubbed it, had no wing mirrors, no fifth gear, no power locks, no power steering, no heating, and no air-conditioning—basically it was an engine with wheels. And what an engine. Top speed of approximately fifty-five miles an hour, at which the noise was unbearable—a high-pitched whine like a jumbo jet about to take off while stuck in first gear. Conversation was all but impossible above fifteen miles an hour.

But it was cheap. We worked out on the way to the first gas station past the airport that, on a daily basis, it was actually less than the cost of a Sydney latte for each of us. This was the fact we constantly mentioned in order to justify our clearly ridiculous decision to rent such an inappropriate car for a vacation that would involve a major drive on all but one of the days.

As I got out of the Crapolla at the gas station I asked Jon, "Leaded or unleaded?"

"Don't know," he replied.

I turned and asked the strangely smiling attendant who was approaching us.

"That will be leaded gas you'll want for that," he said, nodding at the Crapolla.

"Excellent," I replied. "Fill her up with leaded, please."

"We don't sell leaded gas."

"What do you mean you don't sell leaded gas?"

"No one on the island does—no money in it anymore."

"But I've just rented a car that only takes leaded gas."

"Bet it was cheap," was his unnecessary retort.

There are in fact some stations that sell leaded gas on Tasmania, but it did mean we had to take some pretty bizarre routes to get to even the most popular places. Still, the island is so stunningly and consistently beautiful that neither of us minded going on winding routes. After all, it was all good thinking time.

The week was everything I had hoped for and more. On one hand I was sad when it came to an end but on the other I was itching to get back to Kate and the family. It's all well and good running away from your responsibilities every now and then, but, for me anyway, it is not a healthy long-term strategy. I didn't want to be happy by constructing a life *away* from my family; I wanted to be happy with the day-to-day reality of my lot—warts and all. The trip had not only been brilliant in its own right, it had also served to remind me once again how lucky I was to have such a gorgeous brood. I missed them and wanted to get back to properly start my new life with them.

Before I flew home to do so I had a few hours on my own in Hobart, Tasmania's capital city—Jon had flown to Melbourne in the morning and my flight to Sydney wasn't until the evening. Aware that I had taken a week off my training for the Bondi to Bronte Ocean Swim I took the opportunity to visit the Hobart Aquatic Center. It's incredible to a Londoner that a small city like Hobart has such an amazing facility: huge, clean changing rooms, Olympic-sized pool, separate kiddie pool and play area, pleasant café—the works.

I ground out twenty minutes of continuous freestyle and although it half-killed me to do it, and my style was nonexistent, I was actually quite pleased with my progress. So pleased, in fact, that I felt it might even be time for me to start doing some of my training in the rough water, as opposed to pools, when I got back to Sydney.

I was also starting to lose weight. The walking and swimming were taking effect. My trousers were sufficiently looser that I had to tighten my belts, and my face was noticeably changing shape.

It was becoming less of a face within a face and more of just a face. Still a pudgy one, but not a total porker. I was encouraged and as I dug into a three-course lunch to reward myself, I took stock.

I hadn't been off work long enough to actually achieve anything but I was in good spirits and keener than ever on the experiment ahead. I had done a lot of thinking—self-indulgent, pompous, and pretentious thinking—but thinking nonetheless. I had started on a number of projects that were important to me—over and above the swimming. I was drawing and writing, I was genuinely starting to bond with my children (when I wasn't going on vacations without them), the surfing was improving in leaps and bounds, and I'd even started reading again—a passion that work pressures had long since squashed.

A feeling of enthusiasm and optimism swept over me. I was incredibly lucky. I had so much to be grateful for and so much to look forward to, so much I wanted to do and experience. At that moment I felt so alive I never wanted to waste another second of my life. I wasn't just going to be all right. I was going to be fantastic. A world-beater.

There was only one problem. I was an alcoholic.

Chapter 16

Tomorrow I'll Be Different

I HAD BEGUN TO suspect that I had a drinking problem about twenty years earlier. Ten years later, on January 23, 1993, I decided to do something about it. As is usually the case with me, this meant buying a book. I was living in London at the time and I took the subway into Covent Garden specifically to buy it on the first day of its release. It was called *Tomorrow I'll Be Different* and it was written by a man named Beauchamp Colclough. I'd never heard of him; it was the subtitle—*The Effective Way to Stop Drinking*—that drew me to it.

Clutching the book like a guilty secret, I traveled home to our flat in Queens Park (Kate and I hadn't yet been married a year—this was before the onslaught of all our kids). I remember that day as if it were yesterday. I was already two chapters in before

I left the subway. When I got home, I immediately sat down, carried on reading, and didn't get up or pause for anything until I had finished. It was exactly 6 p.m. Time for a drink. Except this time (probably the first time in over five years) I didn't get myself a drink. I vowed I wouldn't touch a drop for the next four weeks. I've always been a determined type so I saw the month out. It was, of course, an entirely pointless exercise as within a matter of days I was back to my old ways with a vengeance.

However, my life had permanently changed. Up until that day, I had drunk with considerable enthusiasm and gay abandon every day. From this point on I continued to drink with considerable enthusiasm every day but "worry" replaced "gay abandon." Five years later, Harry was born and I decided to give it another shot. Again I chose to give up drinking for the month of May 1998. Again I succeeded with ease. And again it was utterly pointless as an exercise, proving nothing apart from the already-known fact that I can be single-minded and determined when I want to. Hours after the month was up (after a friend's wedding), I was completely smashed, singing "Flower of Scotland" to a bunch of bemused strangers in an Ipswich pub after closing time.

Four more years, and a lot of beer later, I was in Australia with a high-pressure job and four young kids. My drinking was still at an enthusiastic level. Not "get uproariously drunk with your pals and hot-wire a car" drinking but "come home from work every night and grimly drink six beers" drinking. I was constantly struggling with it and once again made the monumental (to me anyway) decision to give it up for a month—from October 11, 2002.

Again this was precisely what I did. Again I went back on booze afterward as if nothing had happened. Clearly the month-off thing wasn't working. I was still in denial. I was still pretending to myself after ten years of trying and failing, that I could drink in moderation. I would constantly justify my behavior to myself and others with ludicrous logic: "Well, I may have said I was only going to have one, but six isn't that many, and it's not like I've got a problem." "Of course I shouted at the kids, but anyone would do the same, they were being annoying." This was the type of junk Kate had to listen to every morning as yet again she shouldered the burden of looking after the kids and running the house alone with no help from her husband.

This time my epiphany wasn't long in coming. It came in the form of a rugby match shortly after my return from Tasmania. The New South Wales Waratahs were playing the Canterbury Crusaders in the Super 12 tournament. It was *the* match for the Waratahs. Although the Crusaders were runaway favorites, the Waratahs could save their season if they could pull off an against-the-odds victory. Something in me sensed they would do it (like when I knew that England would beat the New Zealand All Blacks in 1993).

To cut a long story short, they did do it, and in famously memorable fashion—a replacement kicker (take a bow, Shaun Berne) striking a beauty from fifty-five yards out in the last second of extra time to steal it at the death. Amazing, wonderful stuff. None of which is the point. Although it was one of the most dramatic games I have ever been to (and I've been to a lot), it is not the rugby or the result that I remember, but my drinking.

You see, I had made a promise to myself while on a run that morning that I wasn't going to drink that night. Not for a month but just for that night. I was taking my older son, Alex (as I do to every game—Saracens when we're in England, Waratahs when we're in Australia), and I had a slight hangover from dinner the night before, so I had plenty of reasons to stay off the booze.

Besides, I wanted to stay off to prove I could. I needed to show myself that I didn't have to drink.

As I approached the bar in the stadium to buy Alex a Coke and some popcorn, the voice started in my head. *One won't hurt, don't be a killjoy, what's life for if you can't enjoy a beer now and again? You're such a bloody baby, you're no fun anymore, you're so bloody extreme. Why on earth would you choose tonight of all nights not to drink? No one's going to notice, it's not as if anyone else has asked you to not drink, it's just some silly resolution you made while hung over on a run. You've got to learn to be flexible, give yourself a break, you've earned it, start tomorrow, tomorrow you'll be different . . .*

"I'll have one Coke, some popcorn, and a couple of beers, please."

Hold on, I'm only with Alex, why am I buying two? Well I suppose it will save me from having to line up at halftime. Ten minutes later I heard myself asking, "Would you like another Coke, sweetheart?"

"No thanks, Dad, I haven't started this one yet."

"OK, you just wait here, Daddy's going to the restroom."

"I'll have a Victoria Bitter," I said, on my way back.

Hold on, I've now had three beers. Enough is enough, Nigel. If you stop now then you haven't got a problem.

"Dad, can I have that Coke now, please?"

"Sure, back in a minute."

The voice was back again. *There you go, spoiling a great night with all your self-help bullshit. You're having the time of your life, it looks like the Waratahs might actually do it, and you're whining on about having a drinking problem. Your problem is you should relax, give yourself some credit every now and then, you're a good guy, great dad, it's Saturday night for Christ's sake, have a beer . . .*

"I'll have a Coke and a beer, please."

Berne sent his kick over, the home crowd of thirty thousand went wild, I went to the bar for a celebratory beer. *Not because I need to, of course, but it will pass some time to let the parking lot empty and Alex wants to see the team do their lap of honor. Did I say "parking lot"? Shit, I drove. Now how much have I had? Let's see . . . that's five beers . . . but it was spread out over the match so maybe I'm not over the limit. Definitely shouldn't have any more, but then again I did have a big supper . . . be a shame to waste this one now that I've bought it.*

Alex and I were in fine form when we got home. Alex wanted to tell Kate all about the game. I thought I might as well have a beer while he was reliving the match. Then Alex was in bed and Kate was asking me to come up. "In a minute, darling, I just want to check our e-mail," I said as I thought about the other cold beer I saw in the fridge door. Kate retired to bed; I sank the beer. *What I need to round off the perfect night is a nightcap. Damn, out of beer . . . but there is a bottle of my favorite wine, Pipers Brook Dalrymple Sauvignon Blanc. Probably shouldn't open it just for one glass . . . oh, screw it—I really want a glass—I can always put the cork back in.*

Our e-mails were all old. *Should probably go to bed now . . . but then again, seems a shame to leave the last glass in this bottle. I wonder if there are any porn e-mails in the junk folder. I could just have a quick look while I finish this bottle. "Horny Nurses Hungry for Love"? What's that about then? It's incredible what people will do for money, all these links are amazing. I probably shouldn't actually go in to this site . . . then again, what harm will it do? Blimey . . . that's a bit extreme. Shit, I'm out of wine. Bloody house . . . there's never any booze in. You'd think Kate would make sure there was at least a couple in the fridge. She knows I like a cold beer . . . it's not too much to ask. It's not as if I've got a drinking problem . . .*

* * *

The next morning I decided that I would stop drinking. Not give up for a month, or a year. Stop. Never touch another drop for as long as I lived.

It was a deeply personal decision and because of that I didn't feel the need to change the externals. I didn't walk around the house throwing bottles or glasses out. I didn't ask Kate to stop drinking in front of me. I didn't stop going to the liquor store to buy her wine. I didn't even change my social lifestyle—if people wanted to meet me in a pub, fine. I just wasn't drinking.

A couple of friends mentioned it must have been a relief that I wasn't working as my previous job had entailed a lot of entertaining, inevitably involving booze. In reality this made no difference whatsoever. The *decision* was the key thing. Once I made my mind up it wouldn't have mattered if I had been in a dry monastery or a German beer festival. It wasn't harder or easier depending on the situation I was in. *It just was.* It was similar to the weight-loss deal. Once I'd made my mind up to stop eating badly, the amount of visible temptation became irrelevant. I believed that if my resolve weakened I wasn't going to be saved by not having beer or chocolate in the house—I was either going to stick to my guns or not. In some ways it actually helped to be exposed to temptation. Call me picky, but to my mind not drinking because you can't find a drink is hardly solving the problem. This most definitely isn't to say it was easy. It wasn't.

The voice didn't go away. But I started to tell it to bug off rather than attempt to reason with it. I've reread Colclough's book and feel I have an understanding of my, and I suspect a lot of others', problem. The world can be divided into two camps: those who don't have a drinking problem and those who do. For those who don't, Kate for example, I heartily recommend that they drink as often and as much as they like. I want them to enjoy it. Not just when I'm not around but even in front of me—in fact, especially in front of me. I have no problem with others drinking; I have a problem with me drinking, because it's not about amounts or frequency, it's about your mental relationship with alcohol.

There was a simple question in Colclough's book that got to the heart of this. He asked the reader to imagine a simple scenario: Your best male friend is introduced by you to your best female friend. They get on famously. You really want them to be a couple. They become a couple. You couldn't be happier. They couldn't be happier. You really hope they get engaged. They get engaged. You couldn't be happier. They couldn't be happier. They set a date and invite you to the wedding. At the bottom of the invitation it mentions that it will be a dry wedding. The question is, what would your immediate mental reaction to the invitation be?

Be honest with yourself; you need never tell anyone the answer. If, as it was for me, it's "Oh hell, I don't want to go to Alan and Mary's bloody wedding," I humbly suggest you seek help (there are some contact details at the back of this book).

I didn't want to tell people about my decision—I just wanted to do it. I had obviously confided in Kate, who was amazing about it. For some bizarre reason, I thought she would be angry or dismissive. In reality she was gentle, understanding, and support-ive—on top of being absolutely delighted. Despite wanting to keep it quiet until I had some success under my belt, I was deter-mined to take all the advice and help available rather than simply duke it out on my own with willpower, like I usually did with major challenges. Rather than seeking help from friends who knew nothing about the issue, I sought the counsel of strangers who were experts.

My first trip to Alcoholics Anonymous helped me enormously. I was reluctant, and not a little embarrassed, to go. But immediately upon arriving I felt a huge sense of belonging. Apparently, I was a yeti, basically meaning I was one of the rare problem drinkers who was yet to totally screw up his life, but who had recognized his problem and given up. Normally, alcoholics have to be "beaten teachable," as the first speaker explained it.

It's a double-edged sword, being a yeti. On the one hand it means you possess a certain level of self-awareness and have an iron will. On the other, there is the ever-present danger that you will fall—and when yetis fall, they fall far further than the place they were at before they stopped drinking. For the first time since I had bought Colclough's book ten years earlier, I was meeting people who genuinely understood what I was going through and not only wanted to help, but had the life experience to offer useful advice. It made me doubly determined never to pick up a drink again.

In fact, the whole AA experience was a revelation. I found it had benefit and relevance far beyond the narrow confines of the specific issue of drinking. Although I am not a regular attendee, I find the meetings I have gone to as spiritually rewarding as any religious service I have attended. They seem to me to be one of the few occasions in modern life where people—especially men—are open, honest, and caring with one another, with all the bullshit stripped away. I have to confess to feeling slightly ashamed of the ignorant joking I used to do about AA in my drinking days. But then again, as my dad always says, "There is none so virtuous as a reformed whore" and I don't want to go and completely lose my sense of humor. Suffice to say it worked for me. So far.

Chapter 17

Thomas the Tank Engine

BY THE END OF MARCH the office was becoming a distant memory. My parents had left the country. Tasmania, medical problems, drinking, and seventeen pounds of excess weight were behind me. I was swimming up to twenty minutes of continuous free-style (in a pool, I'd still not started training in the open ocean). I was more committed than ever to the ideal of using this, my fortieth year, in a special and life-changing way.

However, a surprising discovery was nagging away at the back of my mind—I hadn't gotten into a routine. Since my last day in the office I'd never been busier. Many friends told me after a couple of weeks I'd be going out of my mind with boredom, and having never taken time off before I had no idea whether they were right or not. Well, they couldn't have been more wrong. I would have loved the chance to get bored. The idea of waking up and thinking, "Oh shit, what am I going to do with the next twelve hours?" was yet to become a reality. In fact the last time I could remember that feeling was during the long summer holidays when I was at home from prep school and the only thing on TV was soap operas. Thank God for masturbation.

So now that my parents were gone and my vacation was over, Kate and I sat down to discuss how best to organize our regular, day-to-day family routine. Now, I like to believe Kate and I aren't pushy parents. We never set out to do more or "accelerate" our kids' development. We just wanted to do the basics that were expected of a normal family in the local scene. Despite this attitude, there seemed to be an enormous number of fixed events around which we had to plan.

On both Monday and Tuesday the boys went to school and the girls went to preschool. On Wednesday, Alex had band practice in the morning before school, Grace and Eve had swimming at midday, Harry had football after school, and Alex had cricket (in a different location). On Thursday, the girls had Kindi Gym in the mornings and Kate had Pilates in the afternoon. On Friday, Alex had rugby league after school. Saturday mornings were match day (cricket) for Alex; Saturday lunchtime was swimming for the boys. Sunday morning both the boys had junior lifesaving lessons (Little Nippers) at the beach and there was touch football in the afternoon.

And that wasn't the half of it. The preparation for these activities would test the patience of a saint. To go to school they had to have clean uniforms and a packed lunch. To go swimming they had to have dry towels and bathing suits, to play rugby the bloody mouth guard had to be found, and being in the school band meant having to practice the saxophone at home (when?). That's not to mention the homework they needed to be cajoled into doing; the two loads of laundry that had to be washed every day, dried, then folded and put away; the shopping that needed to be done; and the meals that had to be cooked. Oh, and the twins were growing like weeds and needed new clothes and shoes constantly.

It was all a little daunting. *How on earth does anyone find time to have a job,* I found myself thinking. *When the hell am I going to write or train for the ocean swim or have a social life or surf?*

A few weeks into my new life, I discovered that I was utterly exhausted, completely drained in a way that work had never affected me. Work pressure usually energized me; the relentless domestic grind simply took my life force, crushed it, and spat it out. At 5 p.m., just when my energy levels were at their lowest, the "supper, bath-time, homework, bedtime" quadruple whammy would kick in. By 7:30, when most of them were in bed, I'd sometimes need to physically lie down. Nothing that a good night's sleep wouldn't help, I initially thought, but with four kids under nine, the actual number of nights when none of them woke up or needed a diaper change or were ill was currently running at one in four. I was so frustrated I actually worked it out.

I say this not to be a bleeding-heart, liberal, new-age metrosexual, but because it's true: Most men who have a traditional office career haven't a clue how hard their partners work. I know I certainly didn't. A self-help author I know maintains he always says to any man who comes to him with his "I'm going to take a year off to be with the family" story, "Come back in six months when the novelty has worn off and then we'll talk." I was beginning to see his point. Child-rearing is not easier than office work, it is simply different from office work.

Any notion that not having to put on a suit and go to work would mean I was going to have time on my hands was by now completely dispelled. It was a hand-to-hand fight to cut out the space to do anything other than wipe asses or read *Thomas the Tank Engine.*

Not that I was complaining. This situation was precisely what I had wanted. If I hadn't taken the year off I would have more than likely worked continuously until after the kids had left home and never actually experienced the family at this feral level. It scared me that so much life had been going on around me that I wasn't even a bit player in—I was simply unconnected to it.

This year was giving me a chance that most men never get—to throw myself at a different lifestyle. I wanted to immerse myself in it, warts and all. Not just to see how I would cope and what I would learn, but also to grow as a person and be more present in the family I had chosen to be a part of. These self-indulgent musings led me to volunteer for even more trouble. On top of the school cafeteria roster I put myself down to take a reading group on Thursdays. A small step in the life of Bronte Primary School, but a huge leap forward for Nigel Marsh.

Chapter 18

Accidental Encrustations

AT THE SAME TIME as all this "new man" baloney was occurring, I was also getting back in touch with another side of my life—religion. Now, before you put the book down or skip this chapter, please let me briefly explain. This wasn't a new affectation. It was simply a side of my life I had recently let slip. Religion is a subject I have always been fascinated by. So much so that not only did I choose to take advanced classes in it in school, I actually spent three years studying it in college. This led to some interesting job interviews—a degree in theology and an ability to read the Bible in Greek not being on the top of the list of most companies' criteria for new hires. I like to think this goes some way to explaining why I spent the first month after I moved to London sleeping in the back of a car.

Then again, the drinking might also have had something to do with it. But religion just seems too important to ignore. Enough people have gone on about it for long enough for it to warrant at least some investigation. Besides, if any of it is true, then it's far too important to leave to the "experts" (especially given that I can't open a newspaper without reading about yet another clergyman up for child abuse or some such).

Put simply—what's the point? Or less simply—are we the centerpiece of creation or are we merely accidental encrustations on a tiny planet, helplessly hurtling around within an enormous meaningless universe? I don't want to get too heavy here, but it seems a shame if life's all just about upgrading your car to the latest model or paying off your mortgage.

The perplexing riddle of the purpose of life is perfectly encapsulated by the contrast of two of my favorite quotes.

The first is by the remarkable George Bernard Shaw: "The true joy in life is being used for a purpose recognized by yourself as a mighty one, that being a force of nature instead of a feverish little clump of ailments and grievances complaining that the world will not devote itself to making you happy. I am of the opinion that my life belongs to the community, and as long as I live in it, it's my privilege to do for it whatever I can. I want to be thoroughly used up when I die, for the harder I work the more I live. I rejoice in life for its own sake. Life is no brief candle to me. It is a sort of splendid torch which I have got hold of for the moment and I want to make it burn as brightly as possible before handing it on to future generations."

Danny DeVito, in his role as Larry the Liquidator in the film *Other People's Money,* was slightly more succinct: "The person with the most money, when he dies, wins."

My vote goes with Shaw. But unlike people of genuine unshakable faith, I don't "know" what my purpose is. It has always irritated me that I can't simply sign up for a religion and be done with it. The internal questions don't go away. I've never been able to pretend to believe in order to access the nice comfortable bits of a tradition. I'm fine with "love thy neighbor" but can't for the life of me believe in the virgin birth or water into wine. I deeply admire some Buddhist traditions but can't get my head around reincarnation. Come to think of it, the whole God thing is a bit of a stretch for me as well.

The problem isn't so much God himself, but the people who talk about Him. They always seem to want to claim that they, and they alone, have the answer and everyone else is wrong. It seems self-evident to me that if you were born in Bombay you are unlikely to be a Welsh Methodist and if you were born in the Australian Outback it is similarly unlikely you'll be Greek Orthodox. It seems obvious that location and era have a huge part to play in one's belief patterns. My natural suspicions regarding anyone or any church claiming an absolute monopoly on the truth, combined with my desire to understand the point of life, left me no alternative but to study it for myself. I haven't yet found the answer, but I have got the solution to those Jehovah's Witnesses who come to your door at the most inconvenient moments—just fetch a copy of the Bible in the original Greek and they run a mile.

My search for a religious tradition I could honestly align myself with bore fruit about eight years ago while in conversation with a couple we met on vacation. She was from an Orthodox Jewish family; he was a Quaker. Over a drunken dinner he recounted the tale of their wedding. Apparently his family had "won" and it was therefore a Quaker ceremony, not a Jewish one. Now most people, including me at the time, wouldn't know anything about Quakers apart maybe from a vague awareness that they make oatmeal.

He had to explain their method of worship to get the full flavor of the occasion across. I wasn't sure if he was exaggerating or not, but he claimed that all Quakers did in church was sit in a circle and say nothing for an hour. No sermons, no prayers, no hymns—nothing. In fact, no church, even. Quakers call it "meeting" and insist it is always held in a plain room or hall with absolutely no finery. He painted a wonderfully funny scene of one-half of the congregation—his wife's family—waiting eagerly for the wedding to start and being perplexed and then horrified when before they'd even noticed anything had happened it was all over and people started filing out of the hall.

I don't know whether it was the drinks or the way he told it but I laughed so hard my jaw ached.

Beyond the humor, though, my interest had been aroused. Surely Quakers didn't actually sit around in a circle doing nothing? I was so intrigued that I promised myself that I would find out more about them. Eight years later, I'm still attending Quaker meetings. The Quakers have no desire whatsoever to prove they are right and others are wrong. They simply state that it is their belief that "there is a little bit of God in everyone and therefore everyone is equally worthy of respect and love."

People who properly sign up are called Friends; those who just go to meetings are called Attendees. I think of myself more as a Pretender than an Attender. I've still got too many unresolved questions. However, I find that their way of being and thinking has enormous value. The people I've met through the Quakers almost invariably seem to live up to the aspiration of George Fox, one of the founders of the tradition when he said (350 years ago),

"True Godliness does not turn men out of the world but enables them to live better in it and excite their endeavors to mend it."

Quakers actually *do* something about their beliefs. Wherever I've attended meetings there has always been some announcement or other at the end where details of a demonstration against some social injustice are given or volunteers are asked to staff the soup kitchen for the homeless. This, combined with their philosophy that "a simple lifestyle freely chosen is a source of strength," made them, in my eyes, a remarkable group of people. If the truth be known, they humbled me. Despite the fact that my lifestyle was neither freely chosen nor simple, I found them such a welcome change from the other churches I had experienced that I resolved to keep "Pretending" until I discovered something better.

Anyway, I'm not sure whether it was the sobriety or the religion, but as I got further and further away from my office-slave routine I was starting to gain glimpses of how a family could exist happily as one. The school run ceased to be hell. The relentless grind got steadily less exhausting. I even started to look forward to bits of it—five in a bath doesn't get you very clean but it's a barrel of laughs if you're not on a deadline and you don't mind water on the walls.

When I was working, Kate often used to talk long into the night about me putting in so many hours and her worry that I was turning into a largely absent father. And while that was a completely legitimate concern, to my mind it goes beyond simple time spent with the kids—if you spend so long away from them and so long at work it can actually corrupt your emotional radar. American author Arlie Russell Hochschild argues, "Owing to the religion of capitalism and the emotional draw of a work culture, what many professionals find is it's easier to love work." She quotes a nursery school director to chilling effect: "This may be odd to say but the teacher's aides we hire from Mexico and Guatemala know how to love a child better than the middle-class parents. They are more relaxed, patient and joyful. They enjoy the kids more."

I truly believe this time off work was mending my emotional radar. Work had been turning into my major source of security and engagement. It had gotten to the stage where I'd put more love and care into reviewing a business presentation than I would into reading my own sons' school reports. Now it was my family that was providing the joy and intensity.

Chapter 19

Knock Knock

OF COURSE THE CHANGES I was going through affected Kate as much as me. Luckily, Kate said she was delighted with the change. To have me fully engaged with the kids was a joy not just for them but also for her. We'd been married for ten years and through that time had gone through a number of life stages together, spanning the spectrum all the way from a "young, double-income, no-kids" couple to a "four-kids, no-income, middle-aged, married" one.

Throughout these ten years the one thing that never changed was my unshakable belief that marrying Kate was the best thing I had ever done, indeed, will ever do. Kate, you see, is the kindest, strongest, most intelligent, and beautiful woman that ever strode this planet. Her sisters call her "Perfect Katie"—praise indeed from the biggest bunch of overachievers you're ever likely to meet. People consistently express amazement that she is with me. My dad's speech at our wedding started with the words, "Nigel, I don't know what you've done to deserve her; she's far too good for you. Treat her badly and she'll leave you." Um, thanks, Dad.

Kate also used to work in advertising, and she was far better at my job than I was until I got her pregnant three times and forced her from the workplace. She's a far better parent than me, and now here I was encroaching on her space again. And this time, as with the last, she was being loving and supportive every step of the way.

I don't like talking about it since it makes me sound like a Bible-Belt fundamentalist, but for me our marriage is my life. But it hasn't always been perfect. We have had a couple of rocky episodes. The first was in the very early days of our courting. I was smashed in the company bar, larking around with the boys from the media department after a long day's work, when Kate appeared and joined our group. Ignoring her, I proceeded to tell a joke.

"Knock knock," I started.

"Who's there?" the group replied.

"Kate."

"Kate who?" they asked in unison.

"That's casual sex for you," I replied.

Charming.

It took us a while to get over that one, but when we had I couldn't help but press the self-destruct button again. We were in Florida on vacation when I spied a bungee-jumping site. This was so long ago that bungee jumping was still a very new fad. The venue was on the roadside with a big hand-painted sign saying gatorjump Essentially, someone had filled a small pond with writhing, hungry alligators and placed a large industrial crane beside it. For $200 you could buy the pleasure of jumping off the top of the crane and hurtling—almost—into the pond.

I was hooked and immediately knew I was going to do it. Kate, on the other hand, was equally certain that she wasn't going to. No problem if I'd left it there, but for some inexplicable reason I felt the need to persuade her to join me. To prove it wasn't fatal, I went first.

"Kate, it's fantastic, you've got to do it," I enthused when I got my breath back.

"Sweetheart, I really don't want to do it. I hate heights and, unlike you, it's not another goal I want to mark off 'achieved.'"

"Come on, darling, you'll love it."

"No I won't, I'll hate it."

This mindless argument went on for about half an hour until, unfortunately, I successfully wore her down. Shaking and white, Kate was strapped into the cage and lifted to the top of the crane. Eleven stories up on a small metal platform above a pit full of alligators and a crowd of cheering onlookers is a pretty intimidating place to be, even if you wanted to do it in the first place. I had been terrified. Kate, however, was frozen. The instructor evidently knew exactly how to deal with such a situation.

"Don't worry," he reassured her. "You needn't go face-first like your boyfriend. You needn't go at all. Just turn around and face me. Hold my hands and lean back. Get the feel of it. If you are comfortable with this you can then do it backward. If not, I'll take you down in the basket."

Kate, trusting soul that she is, moved to the edge and did as he asked. But then, rather than ask her how she felt, he simply let go. It's a moment I've long since tried and failed to forget. Kate screamed and desperately tried to grab the edge of the platform. The Californian hippie next to me yelled, "Fly! Fly like a bird!"

I was silent until the bouncing of the rope stopped and the crane lowered Kate onto the mattress beside the gator pond. To my profound relief, Kate was laughing.

"Look," I shouted to the crowd who had witnessed my moment of heartless cruelty in forcing her up there in the first place. "She loved it, she's laughing."

I rushed over to help unclip Kate from the harness. Her whole body was shaking as she emitted sobs—not of laughter, but of abject terror and misery. She was hysterical.

As courting went, I clearly had a bit to learn.

Chapter 20

Single

I LIKE TO THINK I've improved my act a little over the decade or so since that particular incident. Either way, I was loving the time off work not simply because I was learning to enjoy the kids, but also because it gave me the opportunity to spend proper time with my best friend, lover, and partner. And this time I was determined not to screw it up. In fact, more than not screwing it up I actually wanted to do something special.

The perfect opportunity was staring me in the face. By a bizarre coincidence, my good pal Giles was getting married in France in April, precisely a week before Kate's youngest sister, Jane, was getting married in Italy. Giles had asked me to be his best man and Jane had asked Kate to be her maid of honor. Normally if I had been working these would have been just the types of occasions we wouldn't have been able to attend together—if at all. At best we would have taken turns staying behind in Australia to look after the kids while the other one flew in and out in a mad dash.

In this instance, however, I had a cunning plan. I booked a table at our favorite spot for dinner to do the sales pitch. I got the usual sinking feeling as the menus arrived. But a remarkable thing happened. As expected, Kate agonized over her choice of food. What was unexpected was my reaction—I didn't get irritated and therefore we didn't get into an argument. This was an entirely new but welcome way for us to start an evening out. Kate was in sparkling form, I was chilled out, and we were getting along better than ever.

"Look over there, Nigel," Kate said.

"Where?" I replied.

"The table on your left by the window. The blonde," Kate challenged me.

"What about her?" I queried.

"She's obviously single."

"No she's not, she's with her partner," I said.

"They're not together," Kate replied.

"What are you talking about? They are holding hands," I pointed out.

"Doesn't matter. I know they aren't married," Kate insisted.

"You're talking rubbish. Besides, you've never met them," I countered.

"Don't need to—I can always tell."

"Okay, smartass, you've got me. How can you tell?"

"Simple, she's trying to look interested—really interested—when he's talking."

"That's it?"

"Yep."

"Is it that obvious?"

"Always. Women never give their husbands that type of attention."

"My God, that's so depressing."

"Harsh but fair, sweetheart, harsh but fair."

"Well, I need you to pretend to be interested in what I'm about to say."

"Can't promise. I've heard it all before."

"Not this, you ungrateful cow. I think we should go to the weddings. Both of them. Together."

"Love to. Two slight problems, however: We can't afford it and we've got no one to look after the children."

"Wrong on both counts. I've called British Airways and we can get to London and back on the last of my frequent-flyer miles. And Liz and May will look after the kids," I proudly announced. I had it all worked out.

"Liz lives in Scotland, you dork. Who the hell is May?" Kate asked.

"May is Liz's sister. They have been planning a trip to Australia for over ten years. They've agreed to time their vacation over our trip and take the kids to school and baby-sit in return for use of the house and car. It's the perfect arrangement."

Liz was one of the first nannies we'd had in London. Kate and I adored her, and, more important, so did the kids.

Kate looked genuinely stunned. She was silent for what felt like an age before announcing, "Nigel, you've outdone yourself—anyone looking at me now would think I was single."

I spent the rest of the evening filling her in on the details. Not only would we leave the kids behind, we would make an extra adventure of it by driving, rather than flying, across France and Italy between the ceremonies. We had the time that we may never get again. This was going to be our first trip back to the Northern Hemisphere since our move to Australia. We both resolved to make it a second honeymoon.

Rather than getting upset at being left behind, the kids were ecstatic when we told them our plan. Liz had become part of the family and it had been wrenching for Alex, Harry, Grace, and Eve when they had to say good-bye to her at Heathrow. Truth is, they weren't bothered about missing us as they were far too excited at the prospect of seeing and spending time with Liz again.

In fact, if anyone was worried about the trip, it was me. Was I just running away from my responsibilities again like I had with the Tasmania trip? How would I keep up with my training for the ocean race? How would three weeks away from the kids affect my newly formed closer relationship with them? And perhaps most worrying of all, how the hell was I going to get through two wedding ceremonies sober? Then again I wasn't *that* worried.

Three weeks later, as we got into the taxi to the airport at the start of our trip, I couldn't help but ponder the upsides of being fired. Clearly this lifestyle wasn't sustainable for the long term but in the short term it sure as hell beat the crap out of going to the office.

Chapter 21

BA9

SINCE WE WERE FLYING on frequent-flyer miles, we were, of course, seated next to the lavatories at the very back of the plane. Kate was in heaven. I'd never seen her look so relaxed. To just sit down and be left alone without a child tugging or whining at her had sent her into a serene state of bliss. "We must do this more often," she dreamily said to me as the plane taxied along the runway before takeoff.

I, however, was in shock. In my previous life, I'd been lucky enough to do a lot of long-haul travel—all of it at the front of the plane. I've never understood the people who whine about business travel. In my experience, it's simply fantastic. All you could possibly want to eat and drink, seats that are real beds, films on demand from an enormous library, and, perhaps most seductive, an army of pleasant staff paid to make you feel like you are very special and deserve to be treated like an overgrown baby who obviously couldn't be expected to get up to do anything and must have his every wish anticipated and fulfilled for the entire duration of the journey.

"Would you like cheese and port after the meal, Mr. Marsh, or shall I simply pull the fluff out of your belly button with my tongue while you're enjoying the film?" was the type of hostess attention I had come to expect.

I'd been on this plane for at least half an hour and I hadn't even seen a flight attendant, let alone been offered a massage by one. Quite apart from that, the seat was breathtakingly small. I was so tightly wedged in that I had to struggle to move my arm to press the recline button. The response when I did so made me give an involuntary snort.

"What's wrong, sweetheart?" Kate inquired.

"Not only is my seat clearly designed for a midget, it's bloody well broken," I informed her.

"Don't worry, just speak to the attendant."

"I don't think there are any attendants."

"Don't be silly, there are lots of them up there, I'll call one." I hadn't realized that the gruff, scruffy guy who had been joking around with his gruff, scruffy pal during the safety video was the crew for this part of the plane.

"Yeah?" he inquired as he reached the very back of the plane where we were wedged.

"Oh yes, hi—sorry to bother you, but my seat is broken. When I press the recline button it simply goes back an inch or so," I told him.

"Are you trying to be funny?"

"No," I said, with a sinking feeling that I hadn't felt since I was a young man and had been given my own number by directory assistance. (I'd just answered the questions they'd asked me. Name? Address? It was only when they said, "The number is . . . " and spelled out the home number I was calling from, that I realized they didn't mean *my* name and address. Anyway, I digress.) As he returned to the galley, I thought I heard him muttering something about an anchor or banker. Whatever else the flight was, it was also going to be "an opportunity for personal growth," as the Americans say.

But my physical discomfort was soon forgotten. One of my all-time favorite experiences is the view from any plane that is either taking off or landing at Sydney. It actually would be impossible to oversell it. Sydney airport is in Botany Bay. Literally in it. The two runways jut into the water so you have the impression of landing or taxiing on the sea. In its way I find it far more impressive than the old Hong Kong airport experience that every seasoned business traveler talks about.

But that's not the best part. After the plane has taken off it is impossible not to get a picture postcard view, whichever way the plane is flying. On this occasion we took off facing inland and the heart of the city. Within a couple of minutes we were over the harbor, the bridge, and the Opera House. Because of the proximity of the airport to the center of the city, you are always at the perfect height at precisely the right time.

We could see the entire harbor and the northern beaches for miles. We were high enough to get a majestic sense of scale and perspective but low enough to pick out almost every detail. Individual cars, surfers, boats—all were clearly identifiable. The plane then banked sharply to start the long 180-degree turn toward London. This process affords the best view of all, involving a coastline tour of the eastern suburban beaches, near where Kate and I live.

The plane does a gentle arc that takes you from Bondi beach all the way past Tamarama, then Bronte (was I really going to be able to swim that far?), Clovelly, Coogee, and Maroubra, before retracing its path back over Botany Bay. There is a communication tower in Bondi that has an almost religious significance for me. It's sort of my own private Eiffel Tower. If I can see it, I feel I'm "home." This, along with our house, the boys' school, the girls' preschool, and all the various sports fields they play at had all been clearly visible for over ten minutes. They slowly receded into the distance as we climbed to our cruising height above yet another breathtaking sight (the national park below Botany), and I found myself matching Kate for serenity.

Chapter 22

Seventy Dollars

THE FLIGHT TO THE U.K. is one of the longest you can do on this planet—and in economy class miles it feels like it. It takes hours to even leave the Australian landmass. When Kate's mom first came out to visit, the pilot announced, "We are now crossing the Australian coastline" as the plane flew over Darwin. She put her coat on and got her passport ready. Five hours later, they touched down in Sydney. I remember that when we first came out my kids refused to believe when we did the stopover that Hong Kong wasn't Australia. "How can it be possible to have flown for so long and not be where you are going?" my older son reasonably asked. It *is* slightly perverse; you do one long-haul flight, get off for an hour, and then do another.

This time the stopover itself provided more than the usual interest as it was the height of the SARS epidemic. As Kate and I strolled around the Hong Kong airport, we casually wondered if it was totally sensible to be the only people who weren't wearing face masks. My slightly woolly theory was that it had all been overhyped by the media and that if everyone else was wearing masks then by definition we needn't bother. Kate thought this would be of little comfort to the poor unfortunates who would have to look after our four young children if we were to kick the bucket, but before the argument could really get nasty we were back on the plane for the long leg to London.

I don't really want to relive the flight—once was too much. Boring, sustained discomfort probably best sums it up. All capped off nicely by the descent to Heathrow. A more depressing approach I cannot imagine. Miles upon miles of featureless urban sprawl. The flights from Sydney all arrive very early in the morning and the gray dawn light does London no favors. You're always tired by this stage and the vista does nothing to lighten the mood. I'd lived in London for all of my adult life and had wondered what feelings returning would evoke. At this stage I thought it best to put my current emotions down to jetlag and homesickness for the sun and surf of Sydney.

Matters weren't helped by the fact that when we got to the hotel I opened my bag and I discovered everything in it had been soaked through with dirty brown water. Although we were on a three-week trip, I only had one set of smart clothes with me, and I needed to wear them that evening when we were meeting Kate's sister's fiancé and family for the first time at a swanky dinner, given partly in our honor. There was no chance I could get my suit and shirt cleaned in time. Even if I did, I suspected they would still be stained brown and look ridiculous. There was nothing I could do, so I decided to call British Airways.

Now, I've never had a problem with BA. They've always done what I think is a good job in a difficult industry. Besides, I was a platinum cardholder with a truckload of frequent-flyer miles, so I usually got treated with an element of respect. I called the number on the back of my frequent-flyer card and explained my story and circumstances. They listened politely until I had finished and then told me I needed to speak to Customer Service. They couldn't put me through.

I called Customer Service and again explained my story and circumstances. They too listened politely, waited until I had finished, and then told me I needed to talk to Baggage Claims at Terminal 4 in Heathrow. Again, they couldn't put me through. The jetlag was starting to set in and this process was beginning to piss me off. I called Baggage Claims at Terminal 4 and explained my story and circumstances. They also listened politely. However, this time when I finished they said, "How awful, Mr. Marsh. You're a valued customer. You quite clearly need to buy a new set of clothes for tonight. Take down this reference number and quote it when you send us the receipts for a full refund of your purchases." Now this is more like it, I thought.

"Kate," I yelled, "I'm going shopping for clothes. Have a sleep-in. BA has come through. I needed a new suit anyway. Cheers."

I've never liked shopping, but when someone else is paying it tends to give proceedings a certain extra injection of fun. I shop fast and within two hours I was the proud owner of an entire head-to-toe ensemble. I was particularly proud of the Todds shoes, and felt that however posh this new set of in-laws was, I would be more than well enough dressed for the occasion.

I called BA back. "Hi, it's Mr. Marsh again. I've purchased my clothes and have all the receipts and a reference number. Where do I send them, please?"

The nice man told me the address and then added, "As a matter of interest, Mr. Marsh, how much did you spend in total?"

"Let me see, that would be . . . one thousand six hundred and fifty-eight dollars and ten cents."

"One thousand six hundred and fifty-eight dollars?"

"One thousand six hundred and fifty-eight dollars and ten cents, yes."

"Mr. Marsh, there's a seventy-dollar limit."

"Limit on what?"

"Limit on refunds for ruined clothes."

"You've got to be kidding! What type of clothes do you think I could get for seventy dollars and why the hell are you telling me this now, you dickhead . . ."

I'm not proud of the rest so will spare you the details, bar saying that waking Kate up with a cup of tea didn't really cut it when it came to telling her I'd blown three-quarters of the vacation budget before we'd even spent one night away.

Chapter 23

Gloves

WE DECIDED TO GO our separate ways until the function that evening. Not just because Kate was angry with me for wasting all our money and didn't really want to be in the same room as me for a while—she wanted to spend some time with her older sister, Sara. This suited my purposes as I had a swimming routine to keep up. I knew I would be busy catching up with old friends and family over the next three weeks and that there would be a lot of eating, drinking, and partying involved, but I didn't want the socializing to get in the way of my training.

Swimming in London doesn't exactly compare to the ocean pools of Sydney. As a matter of fact, it doesn't even come close to the municipal pool experience of Hobart. The city pool that I ended up in in Crouch End, our old London suburb, made the

Hakoah Club look like the Sydney Olympic pool. Having said that, I had an excellent swimming session.

Just before we left Sydney I had bought a book in an attempt to improve my technique in the water. I never knew there was so much skill involved in swimming well. I just thought it was a matter of strength, will to win, and getting fit. The book was a revelation. Technique was everything. Apparently all the Olympic swimming winners since records began had taken fewer strokes than their opponents in their races. I had to read that twice. *Fewer* strokes. I would have bet my life on the opposite. But there it was in black and white. Fewer strokes. It was all about efficiency of stroke, economy of energy expended, and minimum resistance to the water.

Just as David's advice about slowing down had radically improved my endurance, the book was transforming my technique. I started to try to "swim downhill," chin on my chest, leading with the top of my skull, not my forehead. I no longer splashed my arms into the water but instead imagined I was threading my hand into the sleeve of a suit jacket being held in front of me on each stroke. (Given my experience earlier that day I tried not to think how much that suit jacket had cost while I was doing this.) I wouldn't claim I was pretty to watch, but the improvement was extremely satisfying.

I got back to our hotel in high spirits. Kate was also in fine form, having had an excellent, if jetlagged, day shopping with her sister. I didn't feel it was my place to point out the lack of logic in reacting to losing lots of money by spending even more. As I've already admitted, I don't really understand women—and anyway I was just happy that she appeared to have forgiven me. I thought of it as a sort of absolution by credit card. Suffice to say, we had now both recovered from the experience of Flight BA9 and were enormously looking forward to our evening out with Kate's family and soon-to-be in-laws.

I've always had a fond spot for Jane, Kate's youngest sister, and indeed the whole Turner (Kate's maiden name) family. Jane was the last of the sisters to get married. Kate was to be matron of honor and I was to make a speech at the wedding. All very exciting, but as we'd moved to Australia two years before, we had never even met her intended, Max, or his family. Tonight was the night. Kate looked stunning in a dress that thankfully hadn't been packed in the bag that some baggage handler had left sitting in a puddle at the Hong Kong airport. I also thought I looked great—it would be difficult not to given the amount of dough I'd unwittingly thrown at my wardrobe for the occasion.

As luck would have it, Max and his folks were, and are, delightful. Jane looked the picture of happiness and, best of all, Kate immediately hit it off with Max. The setting was divine, and it is here that I need to add a bit of background. We were having dinner in Max's parents' polo club. Not the polo club where they play (although they do that as well) but the polo club they *own*. You see, it would be fair to say that they aren't short of a penny.

"Wow, she's done well," I said as we arrived and took in the gorgeous surroundings.

"Oil well, more like," Kate replied.

The sisters are a competitive bunch. They would all deny it, but they each have a deep latent need to prove themselves to one another and to their parents. I couldn't help feeling sorry for Kate, as I was clearly a bit of a disaster in the "validation through your partner" stakes. Her other sisters, Sara and Claudia, had also both married hugely successful and nice men. It was Kate's lot in life to have few bragging rights in the husband department. I somehow thought "Nigel has given up drinking and can now do bilateral breathing" might not cut it among tonight's crowd—or indeed with her mother.

Beyond crippling envy, however, I've never had a problem with the superrich. In my—admittedly limited—experience, they've always been humble, thoughtful, and generous. It's the averagely rich who are the nightmares. But then you'd expect me to say that given I've some new superrich in-laws to suck up to.

The hospitality was expertly planned and delivered. They'd clearly done this sort of thing before—nothing over the top or too intrusive, just a number of perfect touches to create the right ambience. Both sides of the family appeared to like each other. The wine was going down quickly (down everyone but me, of course) and before long the room had that wonderful noisy hubbub that signifies a crowd of happy people in a shared mood of energized gregariousness. Sort of like a Quaker meeting in reverse. Everyone talking—rather than listening—at the same time, leading to a heightened group mood. Only peals of laughter and screams of welcome occasionally broke the loud background hum of good-natured banter. When the time came for food it took an age to get everyone seated.

The meal was in keeping with the rest of the evening— elegantly understated but somehow just exactly how you would have wanted it. After the main course a glass was tapped and the place fell silent as Jane and Max stood to say a few words. Max went first. He spoke movingly about his parents and other family members, giving each a present in turn. When he finished, Jane took over the proceedings. She began by thanking each of her sisters. I couldn't see the presents that Sara and Claudia got but from the look on Kate's face the sparkling thing in the little blue Tiffany box she'd been handed met with her approval.

Jane, however, had clearly saved the best for last. She made a delightful speech about her mom, Mary, at the end of which she handed her a small envelope. Mary opened it to find a round-trip ticket on the Orient Express, a trip she had harbored a lifelong dream to make. She followed up this showstopper with another touching speech, this time for her dad, John. Again a small envelope was given. John opened it to discover the keys to a classic white Porsche, which was parked outside. It was the very car he had always dreamed of driving—now he actually owned one. I was oohhing and aahhing with the rest of the guests when to my astonishment yet another speech was started.

I couldn't believe it. This time I was the subject in question. Jane was clearly touched that I had made the effort to fly all the way from the Southern Hemisphere for their wedding. I could only imagine how they were going to show their appreciation. My luck had clearly changed. Perhaps it wasn't so stupid to have bought those clothes after all. The talking stopped and I was handed a small package. My hands were actually trembling as I opened the parcel. I pulled away the tissue to see . . . running gloves. A pair of black cotton Nike running gloves, available in all good sports stores at $25 a pop.

I frantically looked inside each of the fingers for a lottery ticket or a set of car keys or a diamond—anything to elevate my gift to previously just-seen levels. My search was in vain. The gloves didn't come with any hidden extras. I don't want you to think I'm ungrateful; they are nice gloves. In fact I love them. Besides, I've always felt Porsches are overrated.

Chapter 24

Kulfi Ice Cream

WE WEREN'T JUST excited about seeing family. We'd been away from the U.K. for twenty-two months and we had a number of friends that we were dying to see face-to-face, as opposed to the phone and e-mail methods of communication that we had had to rely on to keep in touch from Oz. The face-to-face option involved numerous trips around the city. A congestion charge—a fee for entering central London—had just been introduced, making the traffic even worse than I remembered. The weather was also shit. To cap it all off, there wasn't a beach in sight. In fact, gazing out of the window of the car on one of these journeys, I couldn't help noticing that everyone looked miserable. It was strangely instructive seeing London through the eyes of a visitor. I had thought the city would evoke a homing-pigeon response in me, but the reverse was the case.

I could absolutely see why tourists and superrich residents loved the place. It is, after all, an amazing city. However, it is the reality of what it means for "ordinary" people to live in London that spoils the deal. If you live on the edges of Hyde Park in a house with a garden, a roof terrace, and a nanny, have your own garage, drive a short distance to work where you have a parking space under your office, and earn north of a million dollars, then it is a pretty agreeable place to spend some time. If, however, you live in one of the suburbs in a terraced shack and have to take the Underground to work every day, it is a different proposition altogether.

I began to wonder what my year off would have been like if I had been in London instead of Sydney. Would I have even decided to do it? How much of my decision was really me proactively deciding to take control of my life and how much of it was a lucky accident that I happened to be in the world's most livable city at the moment I lost my job?

Walking the kids to school through the leafy streets of beachside Sydney is quite different from having to drive them through peak-hour London traffic—congestion charge or no congestion charge. What on earth would my big goal for the year have been? There weren't many ocean swims in North London. I obviously could have chosen another goal—I was, after all, a master at making them up—but I somehow doubt that the London marathon, or whatever, would have exerted the same romantic and motivating influence on me as attempting to swim between the two oldest surf clubs in the world (Bondi and Bronte to this day fight over the honor of which one of them is the world's original surf club).

Regardless of how much I love Sydney, though, there is one thing it doesn't do nearly as well as London: curry. Of all the curries I've eaten in Australia—and there have been a lot—not one of them has come even close to the foothills of a decent London curry. I was reminded of this essential cultural distinction when we spent an evening with our good friends Simon and Becky in their local curry house. It was great to catch up with them. The setting was in its own way every bit as perfect as the setting at the polo club had been. Bright white sign outside the restaurant; laminated menus; awful music; greasy pappadams; surly, uninterested staff; and suspiciously crusted pickles served in a little metal lazy-Susan thing. The evening was topped off perfectly by the uniquely English ritual of the London Curry House Pudding Offer.

Every country has a number of its own entirely pointless traditions. In academic circles they are called "standing waves." Things that once used to have a point but which have continued long after that point has passed. The QWERTY keypad is probably the best example. It was actually designed to slow typists down when typewriter technology couldn't keep up with the speed of secretaries of the day. Now computers can go faster than any human hand can type, but we still have the QWERTY configuration.

I can't possibly think what the original point behind Kulfi ice cream was but now no one—and I mean *no one*—eats it. Ever. Unless of course you are so completely drunk that you have no control over your critical faculties. I've long maintained that the London police could do away with the breath test in their bid to catch drunken drivers. Instead of asking drivers to blow into a bag, a simple "Would you like some Kulfi ice cream, sir?" would do the trick. Anyone who showed the slightest interest could be arrested on the spot with absolute confidence.

Chapter 25

Cleaning the Oven

DISAPPOINTING THOUGH London may have been, I was actually pleased we had a few days left in the city as I had a number of things I wanted to do before we flew to France.

One of these was to go to the Quakers. The nineteenth-century historian George Bancroft said, "The rise of the people called Quakers is one of the memorable events in the history of man. It marks the moment when intellectual freedom was claimed unconditionally by the people as an inalienable birthright." I'm not sure I would go as far as George, but for the last eight years whenever I had traveled to a new city I had always sought out the local Quaker meetinghouse if my trip fell over a Sunday. London was hardly a new city for me, but I hadn't been back for a while and I was determined to keep up the tradition on this visit.

The Quaker form of worship is called the Ministry of Silence. Basically, the group sits in a spartan room on wooden chairs for an hour. No hymns, no prayers, no sermons—nothing. At any time anyone can stand up and say anything. You can't go with a prepared speech, you can't interrupt, and you can't respond to what anyone says. Half the time no one says anything and you just sit there for an hour in silence. Utterly ridiculous. The thing is, I love it. It gives me time to think, to still the mind.

An amazing thing happens when you've been quiet for half an hour and someone next to you stands up and says something. You listen to them. Really listen. You don't judge them. You just listen. And when they've finished talking you don't waste energy trying to come up with a response that will make you look good or prove them wrong, you simply think about what has just been said. Maybe for a whole thirty minutes if no one else speaks. It can be a remarkably powerful and enriching experience. Then again, I'm not saying it's easy to do well—stilling the mind can be a real challenge.

The next morning when I went to the Quaker meetinghouse on Euston Road, I was all but useless at it. You're supposed to sit there in silent contemplation and welcome the Lord in. Instead, my mind wouldn't stop racing, thinking about the vacation and weddings ahead. I mean, Jesus, without the kids around Kate and I might even get it on.

Sex in marriage is one of the few great uncharted territories left—a bit like the deep oceans. It's not that people don't talk about it. They do. It's just that they almost always lie. Kate and I are obviously at it day and night but a *friend* of mine has a wonderful story that illustrates a key truth beautifully. His sexual frustration got so bad that he decided to do that most unmanly of things—he decided to communicate his feelings. In a loving and sensitive way, of course. He didn't think it was right or fair that he should be made to feel bad about wanting sex. It was, after all, natural and supposed to be fun. He was monogamous. He loved his wife. He was in good shape (even if I say so myself, although this is a friend I'm talking about, you understand). His belief was that he needed to first ascertain where sex ranked in his wife's priorities.

"Sweetheart, is sex as important to you as, say, a holiday away?" he started.

"No? Okay, how about a weekend away?" he continued.

"No? That's fine, that's fine. A good meal?" he suggested.

"No? No problem, it's important you're honest. Does it rank above a glass of wine?" he asked.

This line of questioning went on until—and I'm not making this up—he got down to "cleaning the oven." At this stage, he got into a serious debate with his wife about whether sex was something she looked forward to more or less than cleaning the oven. She eventually settled on an equal ranking.

Another friend of mine once told me in a deep depression that his marriage was "like running a preschool with a roommate you used to date." Nice.

I brought the subject up with Kate on a number of occasions but it always seemed to end in tears.

"Sweetheart, how often would you say we have sex?" I once asked.

"Do you mean make love?" she replied.

"Yeah, whatever, make love, sex."

"Well, definitions are important or else I can't answer the question properly. I mean, do you want me to count 'assisted wanks' among the number?"

"Er . . . what's an 'assisted wank'?"

"You know, when I'm there but not there, if you know what I mean."

"No, I bloody well don't know what you mean."

It descended from there as the gap between "making love" and "assisted wank" became ever more apparent and hurtful to both sides.

There seemed to be such a fundamental difference between women and men when it came to sex. Men, especially married men with kids, weren't so much pussy-whipped as pussy-neglected. Time and again I would hear stories from friends who'd bemoan the fact that sex was the cause of tension and stress in their marriage rather than a source of fun, excitement, and togetherness.

When I was working, one of my clients had once opened up after a few drinks. "It's always a wearing-down process, Nigel. I make a move and she rejects me. I wait a few days then suggest it again. She rejects me again. I feel resentful and hurt. She feels guilty and pressured. I wait a few more days. Women in the street, anchorwomen on TV, and gargoyles on the top of buildings start to look strangely appealing. We argue. I shout. She cries. We make up and she says something like, 'Oh, go on then, you big bear, I'll let you.' Trouble is, I don't want to be 'let.' I'd like her to want to. I don't want it to be a reward for good behavior or Olympic patience. It makes me feel dirty and ashamed that I want to get my satisfaction. I'd like to be surprised and delighted by my sex life, not depressed and bored."

"Reminds me of what Jimmy Carter, of all people, said," I'd replied, slightly lost for words.

"What was that?" he asked.

"He said that his wife was more understanding and accommodating of his sexual needs in their seventies than she had ever been in their thirties."

"Reminds me of a recent article in a men's magazine," he said. He was clearly warming to his theme and increasingly worse for drink. "In it they asked women and men what were the three words they most wanted to hear. The overwhelming answer from the women was 'I love you.'"

"What about the men?" I asked.

"'Pick any hole,'" he replied.

On the evidence of this Sunday morning's hour of "quiet contemplation," I felt there was a way to go before I made the grade as a Quaker.

Chapter 26

Headphones

THE OTHER THING I wanted to do before we left London was to spend some time with my brother. I've got only one brother—no sisters. Jon is older by two years and had the joy of having the same schooling experience as me except without an older brother to look after him. He's always had the burden of being "the first" and having to watch out for his younger brother.

During our school days, at the end of each term we would have to travel home unaccompanied to wherever the navy had located our family that year. In some cases—when we were living in America or Belgium, for example—this would mean quite a significant journey. Jon would have to be the responsible one while I could mess around and be cute to the stewardesses.

When we got home I would invariably kick a football through a window (or commit some such wickedness) and he would get beaten for it, not me, even when I owned up to the crime. On one famous occasion, he scratched my new metal peashooter, so I took his new peashooter, went into the garage, got a hammer out of Dad's toolbox, completely flattened his peashooter from one end to the other, took a spade out of the garden shed, and buried his now ruined peashooter as deep as I could in the backyard. Cute, huh? It's really a miracle that he didn't continually beat the shit out of me, but he never did. Instead he looked after me. All in all, the best brother a man could hope for.

He also happened to be one of the most naturally funny men I've ever met. It didn't matter what topic we were discussing, he would never fail to come up with a brilliant line or story that I would then use for the next year and get all the kudos for being a natural wit—"He's funny, that Nigel."

As always we met in a pub.

"You've lost weight," he said, as I gave him a hug.

"You've gone gray," I replied.

Jon's in the army and has been for over twenty years. It keeps him trim and he looked fantastic. But gray. Shit, I thought, surely I'm not old enough to have a graying brother.

Meeting in a pub was an interesting choice for an alcoholic. I was still off the booze but couldn't help thinking of myself as a drinker who was abstaining rather than a nondrinker. It's an important mental distinction and I wasn't there yet. It was easier to abstain with strangers or people whom I had never drunk with, but my brother and I had been drinking together since we were twelve-year-olds sneaking cider in the local woods.

I had come to realize that, despite my initial belief that it was only my decision to stop drinking that mattered, not the external influences, I needed to be more careful with the social situations I placed myself in. We could just as easily have met in a restaurant or his flat but instead I'd chosen the one location where all I could do was "not drink." Talk about making it hard for yourself. To his huge credit, Jon didn't make a fuss or pressure me. I still found it a challenge. I started to wonder how on earth I was going to cope with the weddings that were coming up. All my pals would be at one, all Kate's family at the other. On top of that, I had the pressure of having to make a speech at both occasions.

Despite the inappropriate environment, we still managed to have a great night. Over five pints of beer for him and fourteen glasses of apple juice for me (I tended to drink more liquid now that I was off the booze), we covered every topic under the sun—Jon keeping me in stitches for most of the night. He saved the best for last. Given the train of thought I'd had at the Quakers the day before, our conversation naturally swung to sex. Despite my being out of work, Jon and I were at similar life stages, both married with kids. We had a lot of common ground (although of course it goes without saying that he and his wife, like Kate and I, were also at it like rabbits every day of the week). He patiently listened to my description of one of my particularly badly pussy-neglected friends.

"Know what you mean, Nige, but that's nothing compared to Mike," he said.

"Do you mean Mike as in Claire and Mike?" I asked.

"Yeah. They've recently moved to Milton Keynes. She's working hard, the baby's not sleeping, and he claims he hasn't had it for over a year."

"Jesus, he's a reclassified virgin."

"Yep, just qualified last month."

"But that's not much of a story, Jon. I know a couple of men who have recently reclassified," I said.

"No, that's not the story. Because of his lack of action in the sack he had to take matters into his *own hands*—so to speak," he explained.

"Know what you mean, Jon, know what you mean. But I still feel this story doesn't live up to your usual standard," I complained.

"I haven't finished. Last week Claire was entertaining three of her top clients. Basically taking them to a show and then dinner."

"So?"

"Well, thing is the show was canceled."

"So?"

"So she took them for an early dinner and then home for a nightcap. Mike hadn't been expecting them for at least another three hours."

"So?"

"Wait, wait. Be patient. Claire showed them into the house and told them to make themselves at home in the sitting room while she fixed the drinks in the kitchen. She had hardly got the ice out of the freezer when they all came into the kitchen. The head client explained that there was a *problem* in the sitting room. Claire told him not to worry and that she would see to it when she'd done the drinks. None of the clients would move. The head client had a strange look on his face and simply repeated, 'There's a problem in the sitting room.' Claire went into the sitting room to find Mike in his favorite chair, watching a porn movie, trousers round his ankles."

"But surely he would have heard them coming in the door?" I protested.

"Nope, turns out Mike likes doing it while listening to his favorite rock album through the hi-fi headphones. He couldn't hear a thing. She had to tap him on the shoulder to get him to stop. Apparently it made the introductions interesting."

I made a mental note to lock the door in the future.

Chapter 27

Beyblades

SEX OR NOT, THE U.K. part of the trip was over. It was time for us to leave London. Giles's wedding was next. He was marrying a French lass from Provence. The wedding itself was in the village of Trets, just east of Aix-en-Provence, so we had to fly to Nice. Given our financial situation we decided to put the huge price differentials between the different airlines to the test and fly CrapAirline.com. It was a no-frills deal taken to the extreme.

To our surprise, we were both genuinely impressed. There was no pretense about the whole deal. When you fly BA economy you are paying a premium, but for what? When you fly CrapAirline. com there is no pretense and you actually get pleasant staff. Your expectations are exceeded. On BA you can't help hoping that perhaps the seats will be slightly bigger or the service slightly nicer when in reality the reverse is usually the case. Unless you're flying business class, my vote is with the no-frills CrapAirline.coms.

The flight may have been a pleasant surprise but the destination was a different matter. Nice was anything but nice. I've always found the coastline of the south of France to be a massive disappointment. This is not because of unfavorable comparisons with Sydney; I've thought this ever since I went there backpacking as a teenager years ago. It's either horribly spoiled or horribly pretentious. There doesn't seem to be a middle ground.

Because of my career I usually spent a week each year in Cannes and I never ceased to be amazed at how such a dive could manage to attract major film, advertising, and porn festivals. Then again, come to think of it, the porn festival is probably the perfect partner for the town. I wouldn't care if I never had to spend another minute of my life on the Riviera, which makes the juxtaposition of the gorgeous inland countryside all the more surprising and delightful. It is a wonder to behold—all you have to do is drive for ten minutes inland and the landscape is transformed. It reminds me of those city harbors where the water that laps against the port wall is filthy and full of crud yet a couple of yards out the sea is clean and you can see all the way to the bottom. Thankfully Trets is inland—not just inland but positioned at the foothill of Cézanne's favorite mountain, Sainte-Victoire.

We had learned the lesson from my Tasmanian car-rental experience and had rented ourselves a car from the current century. The drive was delightful. We stopped off in a small medieval village for lunch—just Kate and I sitting on a wall by a stream, eating baguettes and cheese. It was the first time we had been away from our children for over eight years. We were alone, no one was tugging at us asking for sweets, no one needed their diaper changed, no one was crying because their brother had changed the TV channel, and best of all we knew that when we got to Trets that evening we wouldn't have to make the kids' dinner and survive arsenic hour. Only one thing was wrong—we missed the kids.

I know this sounds contradictory, but we were alone and relaxed for the first time in almost a decade and we both just sat there on that wall and talked about our children nonstop. I couldn't get the way they get into bed out of my head. They don't get in at the right place like adults. Wearing their little pajamas with rockets on, they leap upside down onto the bottom of the bed and then roll all the way up to the top and then get under the comforter headfirst, before turning the right way around under the bedding and then reemerging the right way up. It's pretty inefficient but at that precise moment the memory was so cute it was breaking my heart.

I started to laugh, remembering the time I was walking downstairs with Harry when without any warning he dropped to his stomach and slid down the entire flight of stairs headfirst before getting up at the bottom and holding my hand again, as if it was an entirely natural thing to do. Kate brought up the time we were having lunch and, as if in a Steve Martin comedy, the mop bucket appeared upside down on the twins' heads with only their ankles and feet showing. It then proceeded to walk across the room with the accompanying sound track of muffled two-year-old giggles.

Finally we could take it no longer and decided to call home to speak to them. Harry answered the phone.

"Hello, Harry, sweetheart, it's your dad."

"I'm not Harry, I'm Beyblades," Harry replied before handing the phone to Grace.

"Go away, Daddy, I don't love you," Grace said.

"I love you, Daddy," I could hear Eve shouting in the background.

"Well I don't. You're a poo-poo head," Grace added, rather unnecessarily.

Alex grabbed the phone. "Have you got me a present yet, Dad?"

Despite the abuse it was lovely to speak to them. When the phone was finally passed to Liz, she confirmed what we had been hoping—they were having a whale of a time. As we hung up the telephone we decided we could allow ourselves to look forward to the wedding itself without feeling guilty about deciding to do the trip without the children.

Chapter 28

Cézanne

WE ARRIVED AT OUR hotel, a restored chateau, in the late afternoon. We checked in at reception, went straight to our room, and opened the shutters that led onto the balcony. The view was breathtaking—an uninterrupted vista of Mont Sainte-Victoire. Giles had arranged for me to have this room not just because I was his best man at the wedding, but also because he knew how much it would mean to me. One of my favorite places in the world is the huge converted railway station in Paris that is the Musée d'Orsay. Kate and I went to Paris the year after Alex was born and I had spent a day there, awestruck by the sheer amount and quality of Impressionist paintings on display in such a unique setting. Cézanne has many works hung in the Musée d'Orsay, among them a number of the more than sixty paintings he did of Mont Sainte-Victoire in his lifetime. And here I was, looking not at the paintings but at the subject itself.

One more thing I had resolved to do in my time off was to teach myself to draw. As part of this process I had bought and studied an incredible book by Betty Edwards called *Drawing on the Right Side of the Brain*. It's actually quite sad. Its central thesis is that most of us halt our artistic development at nine years old. Up until that time, when we draw, it's all in symbolic icons: houses all have doorknobs, and people all have ten fingers. Then one day, at around the age of nine, we realize what we're drawing doesn't look like things in the real world. So we try to draw them realistically and of course when we do they look nothing like real life, *so we give up*.

Betty Edwards has a theory that is not only dramatic, but works. I know because it's worked for me and I was the world's worst, most hopeless case. Put simply, she says when we try to draw realistically, the left, logical, side of the brain keeps piping up and telling us, "Don't be stupid, it's a house you're drawing. Houses have doorknobs so put in a doorknob." Never mind if you can't actually see a doorknob. This happens over and over again with everything we attempt to draw: "It's a car, put in four wheels," "It's a person, show both her eyes." But the secret to drawing realistically is as simple as drawing what you see.

Ignoring what the left side of your brain tells you is there—as opposed to what you can actually see—is the hard part. If we ignore the left side of the brain it becomes almost easy.

Edwards has devised a number of exercises that force you to ignore the left side of your brain. Things like copying upside-down pictures, and drawing without looking at the page. I copied one picture that was right side up and it was awful and childlike. I then copied another that was upside down. To me it just was a bunch of meaningless random squiggles so I simply concentrated on getting down what I saw. When I'd finished and turned it around, I was stunned to see it was a 100 percent accurate and incredibly lifelike and detailed picture of Stravinsky sitting in a chair. It's one of my prized possessions—I can't believe I did it. If I'd known what it was before I started drawing, the left side of my brain would have messed it up for me by saying, "Where is his other knee?" and "What about his fingers?" It's one of those exercises that once you've done, you'll never forget or go back to how you thought beforehand.

Anyway, the reason I mention this is because in preparation for this trip I had bought a book on Cézanne and while sitting on my balcony I read the following quote from the great man: "We must not paint what we think we see, but what we see. Sometimes it may go against the grain, but this is what our craft demands." It can't have been the drink because I was still off the booze, but the profundity of these simple words spoken over a hundred years ago made me want to weep. Cézanne and the other Impressionists had to endure all manner of ridicule and humiliation for their craft before they were eventually vindicated (in many cases after their deaths). The whole situation just yelled at me—we are only here once, don't toe the line and be a timid, whimpering clerk who doesn't follow a dream because he's too busy doing what he feels other people expect him to do.

Then again, perhaps I should take up drinking again if this is what happens to me when I look at a mountain sober.

Chapter 29

Lucky Bastard

I WOKE EARLY THE next morning. I was excited about the imminent arrival of my Bristol friends. One of the upsides of not having to go to an office five days a week is that it gives you more time to appreciate those around you—or indeed those friends who are on the other side of the world. Most of my longstanding nonwork friends come from my time in college. For one reason or another I had lost touch with everyone I'd ever been to school with but had successfully kept in touch with everyone from college. They were an incredibly important part of my life and one I worked hard at nurturing.

For the eleven years before Kate and I departed for Australia, we had spent every New Year's holiday with this group of friends in a variety of cottages in Devon and Cornwall. Apart from being enormous fun, it was an amazing reality check regarding the passage of time. When we first started going, we were all young, slim, not married, and almost permanently addled with drink and drugs.

Then, as each successive year passed, the signs of the inevitable rites of passage became apparent. Someone got engaged, then another married. Incredibly to us at the time, someone actually brought a child one year. And, here's the thing: It was theirs. The last year we went, when we saw in the new millennium, half of us were sober and there were more kids than adults in the cottage. Knock on wood, none of the six couples involved had yet divorced. They were all coming to Giles and Sophie's wedding. He was the last of the group to get married. Indeed, it had been ages since the last wedding, and this was a wonderful opportunity for us all to get together for the first time since Kate and I had moved to Oz.

Something else that had slowly become apparent was that the magnetic effect London had had on us all at the start of our careers had reversed and in the last two years we had nearly all scattered to different parts of the world. Whereas we once all lived within a five-mile radius of one another in North London, we were now all located in vastly different places: Sydney (Kate and I), Provence (Giles and Sophie), Belfast (Ian and Christine), Melbourne (Jon and Jane), and Brighton (Paul and Janine). Only Simon and Becky (Kentish Town) flew the flag for good old London. Irrespective of the distances involved, everyone had made the pilgrimage to see Giles's big day.

I was sharing the best man duties with another of Giles's close friends, Richard, and I'm pleased to say (although I can't claim any credit since Richard did all the work because I was in the Southern Hemisphere) that the day went off as smooth as glass. The service was in the ancient church in the middle of Trets. It would be hard to imagine a more romantic setting. The duties of a best man in France are slightly different from those in the U.K., but the one duty that was the same was the fact that we each had to give a speech.

I'm sure it must be gross vanity on my part, but I have always loved giving speeches. Not so much the preparation, but the physical act of delivering one. I think it might go back to my stand-up comedy days. The thrill involved when it goes well is something I find delicious. Making people laugh and then, best of all, riding those laughs, for me is right up there as one of the best experiences life has to offer.

The only slight hitch in this case was that over three-quarters of the audience couldn't speak a word of English, so at least some of my speech would have to be in French. It would be fair to say I speak more Klingon than French, so this presented something of a challenge. However, remarkably, once I started I found the performing drug kicking in irrespective of language or lack of alcohol, and I had a fine old time prattling on in an accent that would make my old French schoolteacher weep.

The speech, even though I say it myself, was well received and that being the last of my official duties I could well and truly relax and enjoy the rest of the occasion. First I quickly nipped off to find a TV that was showing the Heineken European Cup rugby semifinal. Munster had got through and was playing Toulouse. I badly wanted Munster to win.

Unlike in religion where I couldn't find a particular brand that ticked all the boxes, in sport I had no such problem—rugby had grabbed me at an early age and it has been my passion ever since. The sight of a center breaking through the line with only the fullback to beat is my favorite moment in any sport. Brian O'Driscoll's performance in the first Lions test against the Wallabies in 2001 still thrills me even though I must have watched the game thirty times. The film made of the Lions' tour of South Africa in 1997 is my favorite film of all time. Not just my favorite sports film, but my favorite of all films. Anyway, I found a set and was rewarded by a nail-biter. Munster led all the way until the seventy-fourth minute, only to be cruelly denied by Toulouse with a late score in extra time.

When I returned, the wedding festivities were in full joyful swing. As I expected, it was an even bigger test of my resolve not to drink than meeting up with my brother had been. Over and above finding it strange to be at such a happy occasion surrounded by my friends and not drink, there was the added pressure of my peculiar decision to take a year off.

Although I don't like to think of myself as a "keeping up with the Joneses" type of person, I was worried about my old friends' reaction to my unemployment. After twenty years in an office career it wasn't a simple task to divorce my self-worth from my job—however much I had convinced myself I was no longer going to define myself by my work I was still concerned about what other people might think. Especially my friends. I know this admission makes me shallow but I wanted to appear to them like I'd gotten it all together. (Even though the truth was I was making it up as I went along, and in my quieter moments I was scared shitless of the future.)

It was just too confronting for me to dwell on the reality with my friends and risk being thought of as a sad loser. Just a few months ago, this worry was precisely the sort of thing I would have used drinking to help me get over. Now that social crutch was gone.

Although everyone seemed incredibly supportive of my choice to take time off, I couldn't help suspecting that many of them (especially the women) were simply being polite and had already translated "decided to take a year off" into "poor bastard can't find a job." Some of the men were clearly envious and oversimplified the bright side.

"Christ, you're a lucky bastard, Nige. I'd love to be made redundant. Must be wonderful," was a typical response. I spared them the stories of arsenic hour, Good-bye Windows, and crippling worry about the future. Playing along with the "Nige is spending a year having a laugh and surfing" story was easier—and it made me look good. Or so I thought.

I'm pleased to say my resolve held and I didn't touch a drop. You are not supposed to rely solely on willpower to beat the booze. Whether it is working the twelve steps, having a mentor, using a support network—or in many cases combining all three—you are always advised never to attempt to do it alone. Kate maintains that this is the one area of my life where my hideously black-and-white and determined character doesn't make me a "selfish, intransigent pain in the backside" (as she sweetly put it a few days ago) but instead actually helps me and the family. I take issue with the intransigent pain bit but I feel she may have a point about this finally being a useful outlet for my stubbornness. Whatever, at this stage of my recovery it was all I had.

Being sober actually gave me a different and richer take on the evening. In previous years I would have got stuck into the alcoholic refreshments and tried to be the funny guy all night long. This would inevitably mean a certain tunnel vision and me unwittingly upsetting a number of people along the way. This time I spent the night truly aware of my surroundings and what the people in them meant to me. I felt extremely fortunate and blessed.

Kate looked stunning. Watching her dance and laugh with Becky, Christine, and Jane, I realized again how lucky I was to be with her. We'd been married for ten years. Wonderful years. I made a silent resolution to strive to make the next ten even better. Giles and Sophie were in that blissful state that only newlyweds can be in. I couldn't help but be deeply moved by it all. I had known these people for over twenty years. So much had happened in that time. I said a prayer for Giles and Sophie and for the future happiness of all in the room. I couldn't help wondering where we would be in another twenty years' time.

Chapter 30

Chicken

SINCE I WAS the only guest not sporting a hangover the next morning, I got up early and went for a walk by myself around the foothills of Mont Sainte-Victoire. I took my sketchbook and did a number of shamefully poor pictures of the mountain in Cézanne's honor. Today was the start of the second half of our Northern Hemisphere tour. After lunch in Aix with all the Bristol crew, Kate and I planned to drive to the Italian lakes for a few days before continuing on to Venice for Jane's wedding (and another speech). Neither Kate nor I had been to the lakes and everyone we knew who had been raved about them. The real point of the trip, however, was to have some time alone together.

Bizarre as it may sound, even though we had left the kids behind we still hadn't had much time alone. We were so busy and pleased to be catching up with our friends and family that the subplot of the trip (a second honeymoon) was in danger of being overlooked. We both knew Venice would be as busy as Provence, so this week was our chance to "take a chill pill," as Alex had put it on the phone to me the night before when I'd called him to let him know the Munster result.

Returning to the chateau at midmorning, I found the group slowly gathering for the trip to Aix and lunch. It felt slightly like preparing for the Last Supper. We all realized it might be a very long time before we were together again as a group. Rather than spoiling the occasion, it lent the proceedings an interesting poignancy. I found myself saying the things I wanted to as opposed to wasting the event with mindless chitchat. As Kate and I drove away at the end of the lunch and our French adventure, we both agreed that the trip had already been a huge success regardless of how the Italian adventure went—and indeed the seventy-dollar refund disaster.

To get to the Italian lakes we headed north up the highway toward Gap. It was going to take us two days to get to the lakes, so we put a pin in the map in the vague area of what looked like halfway to decide where we'd stop for the night. Le Monêtier-les-Bains, the pin told us, so Le Monêtier-les-Bains it was. The drive was fantastic—no kids squabbling in the back, no "Wheels on the Bus" on the tape player. Just lovely scenery and no pressured deadlines.

After Gap the highway ran out as we climbed into the mountains. The last town before Le Monêtier-les-Bains was Briançon, which proudly and repeatedly announced itself on gaudy road signs as "the highest town in Europe." Briançon appeared to have little else to recommend it. A grubby urban blot on the otherwise gorgeous surroundings, it even had its own Burger King and KFC for good measure.

As our chosen village was only nine miles farther up a side road, we began to doubt the wisdom of the "pin method" of accommodation selection.

We couldn't have been more wrong. Le Monêtier-les-Bains was a delightful Alpine village. We couldn't believe our luck. I've no idea why it is so unspoiled, but everything from the church to the High Street to the picture-perfect little inn we had booked made us immediately fall in love with the place. The village was surrounded on all sides by the most breathtaking mountain range. It seemed a shame we were only going to be there for one night. Having quickly unpacked our overnight bags, we went for a walk to get the most out of the place before night fell. Back at the inn, against the pleadings of Kate, I went to the front desk and called the kids.

The call was a game of two halves, as the sports commentators say. Alex came to the phone first and was full of excitement about that weekend's rugby match. His team—the Clovelly Eagles— had won and Alex had scored a try and got two conversions over. I tried to control my fatherly pride and while congratulating him also talked about how it was a team game and tackles were more important than tries. No pretending, however, I was fairly bursting with joy at his pleasure in the whole day.

Did it matter that I wasn't there to watch him? I tried to justify our choice by remembering that I hadn't missed any of Alex's previous matches and that in a rugby-playing career spanning fourteen years, my own dad had watched me just once, and then his only comment after the game was, "You dropped the ball twice." Having finished with Alex, I asked him to pass the phone to Harry.

"Hi, Harry, it's your dad."

"I'm not Harry, I'm Punch Buggy Green."

"Oh, okay, sweetheart, what did you do today?"

"Nothing," he replied. "Dad?" he inquired, in that cute way kids do with just the inflection at the end of your name.

"Yes, Harry."

"I'm not Harry, I'm Punch Buggy Green."

"Oh, sorry. Yes, Punch Buggy Green?"

"Isn't it funny how they have one word for *two* things?"

"What do you mean, sweetheart?"

"You know, one word for two things."

"I don't understand, darling."

"You know. Like 'chicken.' 'Chicken' meaning an animal and 'chicken' meaning a sandwich."

"That's not two things, darling, chicken is the animal that we eat in sandwiches."

Now at the time that felt like a perfectly normal, and indeed helpful, fatherly thing to say. Writing this now, months later, having the hindsight of the reaction I caused, it just seems bloody stupid. If I could take it back I would. But then again, one more vegetarian won't hurt, either.

Harry, or Punch Buggy Green as he was at the time, went silent, then started crying quietly, then walked away from the phone. It's difficult to accurately describe how much of a shit you feel when you've just made your five-year-old son cry and you are fourteen thousand miles away from him and he won't come back to the phone.

"How was that?" Kate asked as I returned to our room.

"Oh, fine," I lied. "Harry is Punch Buggy Green today. He sends his love."

Chapter 31

Bored

WE SET OUT EARLY the next morning and were rewarded by the most beautiful drive either of us can remember. The route across the mountains and over the French-Italian border was spectacular but not for the fainthearted—lots of unfeasibly narrow roads with hairpin bends overhanging sheer drops into seemingly bottomless ravines. Not for the first time, I congratulated myself on having learned the lesson from Tasmania—I wouldn't have fancied the drive in the Crapolla.

But things changed abruptly once we came down the other side of the mountains. The drive from Turin to Milan was a real eye-opener. Just because it was Italy, I had naively assumed it would be all vineyards and history-soaked landscapes. The disappointing reality was that it was little more than a desolate industrial wasteland. We stuck to the highway and made as fast a time as we could. Our destination was a place called Bellagio.

Bellagio is on Lake Como and it is world famous for two things: George Clooney has chosen it as the location of his get-away-from-it-all vacation home, and it is the location of the Villa Serbelloni hotel. The Villa Serbelloni is one of those fabulous hotels that is a destination in its own right. Unfortunately, Kate and I neither knew George Clooney nor had a budget that could accommodate the Serbelloni's butt-clenchingly expensive rates. Instead, we stayed in the hotel next door—*looking* at the Serbelloni.

Despite the lack of a hotel swimming pool, I was determined to maintain my swimming training—especially in light of my recent progress—so that afternoon I decided to try my luck, stroll across the road, and pretend to be a guest at the Serbelloni. Heart pounding, I walked with as much outward confidence as I could muster through the reception area and followed the signs to the health spa, a splendid, ornate affair in the basement of the main hotel building. Rather worryingly, there was an officious-looking uniformed lady behind an oak counter just inside the door to the spa. I decided selective truth was the best policy.

"Hi, I've come to use the pool," I said, looking her straight in the eye.

"Certainly, sir. Welcome to the Serbelloni Health Spa. We haven't seen you at the hotel before, have we?" she asked.

"First time in Bellagio. My wife and I just arrived this afternoon."

"And you are staying . . . ?"

"For four days," I interrupted, before she could ask which room I was in, as my policy didn't extend to telling a direct lie. "We've a wedding to go to."

"Oh, how exciting. The tent is being erected as we speak. Do you know the bride or the groom?" she asked.

Hold on, I thought, I had no idea there was a wedding at the hotel. This clearly was my chance.

"It's my sister-in-law who's getting married. I'm a little nervous about the speech I have to make," I replied truthfully but entirely misleadingly. "I was rather hoping to fit a swim in every morning we're in Bellagio. What time do you open?"

"Six in the morning, sir," she replied, handing me a luxuriously fluffy embroidered towel.

From that moment on she clearly believed I was a wedding guest at her hotel, and every morning she greeted me with as much enthusiasm and warmth as the Kindi Gym instructor had before Grace ruined my chances. I rationalized my behavior with the excuse that I wasn't doing anyone any harm and I hadn't actually told a lie—I was indeed staying four days and going to a wedding. Just not at their hotel, or in Bellagio. Besides, it wasn't the worst case of bluffing I had been guilty of. My Serbelloni confidence trick was positively insignificant compared to the sports instructor "career" I manufactured when I was working in London.

There was a sports club just around the corner from the office where I worked and I got it into my head that if I played my cards right I could earn some extra money as a squash coach. Bizarrely, the fact that I had never coached anyone in my life, been coached myself, or indeed even played for a team didn't deter me. I drew up a couple of ads to stick in the sports club reception area and went to find the manager.

"Hi, I'd like to speak to the manager, please," I said to the track-suited hunk at the front desk.

"You're speaking to him."

"Oh, great. You've got three squash courts here and I was wondering if I could use them to give a few lessons," I said, passing my ad across the counter.

"What've you got in mind?"

"Just sticking these ads up on your bulletin board and splitting any business I get with you sixty-forty. If I get too many clients and start jamming up the courts I'll stop any time you like."

"Can't see why not," he said.

And that was it.

Giving the lessons, however, proved slightly more problematic than getting the gig. My ad had rather ill-advisedly read: "Call Nigel Marsh for one-on-one squash sessions, relaxed, friendly. Flexible times to suit any schedule. All standards welcome." Again, no word of a lie but entirely misleading. The last sentence was the biggest problem. I started to get calls. A lot of calls.

The children and beginners were no trouble. I actually think I helped a few. It was the people who were clearly better than me that were the challenge. A couple of them were in line for national trials—I hadn't even made the school team. It would be obvious by the warm-up if I was in trouble. Whack, whack, whack—they would smash the ball with a flawless swing and inch-perfect precision down the wall.

"Okay, couple of things we can work on there," I would say in my best Zane impersonation.

"Excellent—what?" my client would ask eagerly.

"I think we need to work on your swing and precision," I'd reply.

I'd then spend thirty Monty-Pythonesque minutes getting them to go through a variety of routines that I had devised precisely for clients such as these. Among other things, these involved them trying to hit the ball back to themselves ten times in a row while blindfolded or playing left-handed or standing on one leg. On one occasion I even made someone play with a table tennis paddle. Anything but play me. All the time I would nod thoughtfully and wisely, but vaguely, commenting, "Interesting, let's try that on your backhand," or "I want you to relax more at the moment of contact."

Luckily for the future of English squash, after a couple of months the stress of constantly fearing that I would be revealed as a fraud led me to "resign" from the post and concentrate on my office job. I was a few hundred dollars richer but, more important, I had learned firsthand the truth of the cliché that if you wear a doctor's coat with enough confidence you can walk around a hospital for a surprisingly long time before anyone will ask you who you are or what you are doing.

My bluffing ability was hardly at the level of that guy Leonardo DiCaprio plays in *Catch Me If You Can,* but I was rather glad of the opportunity it was giving me now, ten years later in Bellagio, to continue my swimming training. Kate had a slightly different attitude toward my bluffing, maintaining that perhaps it wasn't such a bad thing that I hadn't spent all that much time with my kids over the previous years, as who knows what kind of scams they'd be running now if I had.

The swimming itself continued to go well. Now that I had found my "jogging pace," as David called it, it was more a matter of practice than learning. I found I could now easily swim for twenty minutes or more without stopping. I was relaxing and concentrating on my style. I was even starting to get comfortable with bilateral breathing. Once or twice I actually enjoyed it. I was starting to feel confident about making the move to ocean swimming when we returned to Australia.

Doing Bellagio—and indeed the whole vacation—"on the cheap" had reopened my eyes to an entirely different way of living and consuming. I realized I had practically been pouring money down the drain on a weekly basis during my recent working life. If I had been working when I'd gone to Tasmania I would have spent three times the amount I ended up spending, yet I very much doubt we would have enjoyed the week any more. Similarly, if I had been working during this European jaunt we wouldn't have been staying at the Hotel Florence invading someone else's pool, but I genuinely believe we wouldn't have enjoyed Bellagio any more by staying somewhere more expensive. Then again, wondering where we would have been staying on this trip if I had still been working was kind of academic, given that I wouldn't have had time for such a vacation with Kate if I had still been working.

It was as if I'd been living in a yuppie zone in which I bought what was expected of someone in my position without pausing to question whether it represented good value. Looking back, I realized I had got into the habit of having $90 haircuts and drinking $35 bottles of wine. While I no longer drank, I had just had my hair cut for ten bucks and I'd been very pleased with it when I walked out of the barber's. I suspected if I was still on the booze I'd be drinking cheaper wine and enjoying it just as much.

This is not some pathetic "Isn't poverty great?" mantra. It isn't; poverty is shitty—it ruins lives, breaks up families, causes wars, and generally squashes the human spirit. I'm not talking about poverty. I'm talking about overprivileged people losing their sense of perspective. A few months before I had quit work, I had gone to a cocktail party in a gorgeous house overlooking Bronte beach.

Within five minutes the host had started complaining about the house. Not "I'm a lucky bastard who has a house sixty seconds' walk from one of the nicest beaches in the world" but "We're finding the noise on the weekends distracting." Even at the time I remember thinking, *Get a grip, you jerk-off.*

Looking back, I could recall hundreds of dinner parties where we all sat around and bemoaned the fact that we probably couldn't afford to send our kids to private school. So what? Send them to a state school like everyone else. The problem, it seems to me, is that some people have never, literally never, had to struggle. Be it because they have always worked in the city or have rich parents or made a fortune on a house—whatever.

After a few years of not having to agonize about money they cross an unseen line where they come to subconsciously believe that they deserve and are owed the good life by right. Then, when something happens that means they can't automatically have exactly what they want, they talk about it as if it is a tragedy and other people should care. I've lost count of the number of conversations I've been in where people who work in the financial community have complained about the size of their bonuses since the recession. The fact that even these pared-down bonuses were four times the size of the annual wage of a general practitioner, or the fact that they had enjoyed ten years of "really good" bonuses, didn't seem to register. It was too long since they'd crossed the invisible line of "I've a right to this lifestyle."

Similarly, having to move to a more humble house because you suddenly haven't got as much money is not a tragedy. It's not even a shame. It's life. Count yourself lucky you had a nice one in the first place. This may sound harsh, but I mean it. Although it hardly ranked in terms of real hardship, Kate and I were going to have to move to a cheaper, smaller place down the hill when we got back to Oz. We would have moved earlier, before this trip, but we had a fixed-term lease that we couldn't get out of until the end of May.

A number of friends were appalled at the fate that was befalling us and were genuinely sympathetic. All I could think was, *It's Clovelly—no problem, another wonderful Sydney beachside suburb. Our rent would be double to live in a place half as nice in London. We don't really need the spare bedroom. Anyway, it'll do the children good to share.* Kate thought this attitude was simply an obvious case of retrospective justification, given my situation. I prefer to believe it was a brilliant flash of insight and a searing indictment on the professional classes in the developed world. But then again, I still tuck my undershirt into my underpants if she's not watching.

Our stay in Bellagio was everything I had hoped it would be—I got bored. Properly bored. It happened on the second morning. To start with, I got up when I woke up, not when a twin smashed me in the nose with a Teletubby. When I came back from my swim I found a note from Kate saying that she was going shopping and would meet me for lunch.

I had a bath, a very long bath. After that I ordered a latte and freshly squeezed orange juice, sat on the balcony, and read the newspaper in that way which I never thought I'd ever do again—cover to cover without interruptions or rush. Then I did a drawing. Then another. Then—and it is difficult to adequately describe how wonderful this felt—I actually found myself thinking, *What on earth shall I do now?*

I didn't want to go back to bed. I didn't want another bath or to read another paper. I couldn't surf, I wasn't drinking, I didn't have a job to go to, there were no kids to look after, Kate was out, there were no friends to socialize with, no family to accommodate, no one had our telephone number, and my mobile had been off for days.

It was such a totally alien experience—pure bliss, in fact. I sat on the balcony in a state of semishock, watching the ferries arrive and depart from the terminal below. So this is what it was like to be properly chilled out. It occurred to me I was finally doing what everyone probably thought I'd been doing the whole time—sitting on my fat, beautifully healed butt, doing nothing. It wasn't a lifestyle I could afford in the long term—or even the medium term, come to think of it—but as a short-term strategy it definitely got my vote. Besides, it wouldn't last long anyway, as we were soon to set off for Venice, but I damn sure was going to revel in it for as long as I could.

Chapter 32

Veniceworld

SURE ENOUGH, BEFORE I had time to slide from bored to comatose (a state I had been eagerly looking forward to), we were packing to leave Bellagio. But the disappointment of leaving was more than compensated for by the prospect of Kate's sister's wedding and our first-ever trip to Venice. It was a surprisingly easy drive and upon arrival we immediately made our way to the airport to return our rental car. We had hardly unloaded our bags when a handsome guy in a suit came up to us and introduced himself in impeccable English.

"Are you with the wedding party?" he asked.

"Er, yes. I'm Nigel and this is Kate," I told him.

"Excellent, we've been expecting you. Please leave your bags with my colleague and follow me."

Rather uncertainly we followed him to his car as a porter loaded our luggage onto a cart.

"Please," he said, gesturing to the backseat as he held open the door, "it is less than two minutes' drive to the boat that has been arranged to take you to your villa."

"Villa?"

"Yes, it is one of my favorites. You're on the Grand Canal right opposite the Guggenheim museum. Both St. Mark's Square and the Accademia Bridge are within five minutes' walk if you want to see any of the sights before the wedding."

Obviously the wealth of Jane's soon-to-be in-laws was matched only by their generosity. Now, I consider myself to be fairly widely traveled but in the last forty years nowhere has had such a dramatic effect on me as Venice. I don't know whether it was because we were experiencing it first-class or because I was totally chilled after Bellagio or simply because of the uniquely wonderful place it is, but Venice stunned me. Just the boat ride from the airport would have been enough. I found the whole thing difficult to take in.

I spent a year living in Little Venice in London and all I can say is the person who came up with the name for that particular piece of North London deserves a marketing medal. Located between a number of London's busiest roads, Little Venice is not even a proper suburb—it's basically the few streets that border the intersection of two narrow polluted canals. More "Open Sewer" than "Little Venice," those canals are fenced off from the general public so you couldn't access them even if you wanted to. Little Venice is *nothing* like Venice.

Venice is one of those globally iconic destinations that doesn't disappoint. I remember, in contrast, my utter astonishment when I saw the Egyptian pyramids in person.

"Oh look," Kate had said, "it's a miniature Sphinx."

"Madam, that is the Sphinx," our guide rather huffily corrected her.

We couldn't believe that the minuscule cat at the bottom of the pyramid was the Sphinx. It is amazing to me that every postcard ever taken of the Sphinx and the pyramids has deliberately used perspective in such a way as to give the entirely misleading impression that the Sphinx is almost as big as the pyramids themselves.

Venice, on the other hand, was *better* than the postcards. It really is a city in the middle of a lagoon, with canals instead of roads. If that isn't enough, it also has the most incredible collection of art and historically significant architecture anywhere on the planet.

The only downside I experienced in the whole week we were there was on the second day, when I got stuck, literally stuck, in the middle of a guided group of tourists on a crowded, narrow walkway. Within minutes, the awe-inspiring city I had fallen in love with took on a "Veniceworld" feel. I became a member of a herd. A rather overweight, bored-looking herd that was being systematically shepherded from one "attraction" to the next. At times I half-expected them to complain that it wasn't a very good theme park and ask where the rides were. This short blot apart, it turned into one of the most fabulous weeks of my life. Kate was largely busy with arrangements for her sister's wedding, so during the days I was free to wander the city by myself.

Apparently Venice has over four hundred bridges—I swear I must have walked over all of them. Though the fact is I could have stayed for another week and done it all over again. I constantly felt guilty giving such a short bit of my time to each of the wonders I came across. I could have spent a week in the

Scuola Grande di San Rocco alone. The guidebook I had bought told me I could never be prepared for it until I saw it. And the book was right.

Basically one man—Tintoretto—spent twenty-three years of his life creating works of art to adorn the walls and ceilings of the famous building. Every painting is a masterpiece in its own right—and he did over fifty of them. I had mixed emotions. On the one hand it was wonderful and awe-inspiring, and on the other utterly depressing. My own efforts were lame by any standards, but by Tintoretto's they were pathetic, tragic, and pointless.

I consoled myself with the memory of Harry's response every time he saw one of my sketches. "Daddy, you're an artist!" he would shout enthusiastically while pointing in wonder at my latest scribble—irrespective of how appalling the particular drawing in question was. He was genuinely delighted and amazed at my output. Kate might roll her eyes whenever I showed her my most recent picture of her (invariably looking like an eighty-year-old witch done by Picasso on an off day) but to Harry, for the time being, anyway, I was Tintoretto in board shorts.

This memory served not only to make me smile but also to ache for Harry and his brother and sisters.

"God, I miss the kids," I said to Kate.

"Me, too," she replied.

"Wouldn't it be fabulous to bring them here and show them all this?"

"Fabulous—and entirely unrealistic," she remarked. "Unless you go back to work we won't be able to afford to take the kids anywhere but the local park."

Much as I hated her for spoiling the moment, I had to admit she had a point.

Chapter 33

Back by Ten

HOWEVER, I WASN'T in Venice to sightsee—I was there for a wedding. My wife has three sisters, or the Macbeth witches, as I prefer to think of them. It was the youngest one who was getting hitched this time. At our own wedding, Kate's dad, John, started his speech by saying that the only time in his life when he wasn't interrupted was when he was giving a speech at one of his daughters' weddings. I wondered what his emotions were now he was finally rid of them all.

To have four grown-up daughters is an achievement to rival Tintoretto's in my book. I only had two daughters who were barely three and I could hardly cope with the *thought* of the years ahead. What on earth I was going to do when they actually started maturing, God only knows. It's a man's worst nightmare—when your darling baby girls start to have boyfriends.

Every father knows from his own shameful personal experience that these little bastards will have one, and only one, thing on their minds, no matter how nice and polite they are to the crusty parents. It's just human nature. At the tender age of nine, my father promised me two hundred dollars if I didn't smoke one cigarette before I was twenty. I had seriously toyed with the idea of offering Grace and Eve $10,000 each if they didn't have sex until after I was dead. Then again, the day after my father made his offer I went out and smoked my first cigarette, so perhaps it wasn't the most effective policy.

One of my Australian friends has two grown-up daughters, and one day, after a glass or two, he told me how he would swap all his wealth and success for the chance to bring up his daughters again—differently. He got steadily more depressed as he filled me in on the details.

"I thought I could manage them like I managed my business," he told me. "I had it all mapped out. Whenever my elder daughter had a boyfriend visit the house to take her out, I would make sure my wife delayed her so I could be alone with the lad in question."

"Why?" I inquired.

"So I could fill him in on the ground rules," he replied.

"What were the ground rules?"

"Well, it was more a rule than rules. I simply told each one of them that if he didn't have my daughter back home by ten o'clock that night then I would have him killed."

"Bloody hell, that's ridiculous. How old were these poor bastards?"

"Oh, anywhere from fifteen to nineteen."

"And that's all you said?"

"No, I also said I'd have them shot if they told my daughter about our little chat."

"So what happened?" I asked.

"Well," and here his voice got quiet and mournful, "they all brought her back by ten o'clock."

"A result of sorts, I suppose."

"No, it was a total disaster. I didn't realize it at the time, but it messed her up for life. She couldn't work out why no one liked her enough to spend any time with her and always cut her dates short. Unbeknownst to me she tried everything—and I mean everything—to make them like her. None of it worked, of course, and they all brought her back by ten. She's never actually gotten over it. Twenty years later and she still hasn't a clue how to relate to men. And it's all my fault."

"But what about your other daughter?" I asked.

"Worse," he said.

"Worse? Bloody hell, how could it be worse?"

"I did the same drill on her. Panned out slightly differently, however."

"How differently?"

"It was her first boyfriend. I got him in my study and gave him my speech. Half an hour later my daughter was yelling in my face, calling me a fascist pig, Stalinist sexist, and a whole bunch of other politically confused and extremely unpleasant stuff. Turns out the ballsy little bastard had gone right out and told my daughter what I said to him. She left home and went to live with him to spite me. Had two kids out of wedlock, then left him. But even worse was that she told my elder daughter, who then worked out why none of her relationships had worked. She challenged me on it and I admitted what I'd done. She hasn't spoken to me since."

Tragic though his story was, I was glad to have heard it. Ever since, the thought of unwittingly ruining Grace and Eve's lives by being a loving but utterly useless father has been even more painful than the thought of them being pawed by a succession of horny teenagers. Hopefully when dating time comes for my own daughters it will mean I have at least *some* balance and sensitivity. Or, more truthfully, that I'll have the sense to ignore my instincts and listen to Kate instead.

Chapter 34

Offshore

As far as I could tell, John had done a slightly better job of parenting than my Australian friend, but nevertheless I'm sure his fatherly duties had brought with them a certain amount of stress. The ending of this particular era was clearly a huge rite of passage for him, and the occasion—especially given the location—was filled with significance. Jane and Max had really pushed the envelope with the arrangements. The night before the wedding there was to be a white-tie dinner for 150 guests in a private palace on the Grand Canal.

It had been a while since we'd had the polo club experience in London so both Kate and I had forgotten the type of company the happy couple mixed with—perfectly nice and all that, but just so totally alien to our normal frame of reference.

Models, bankers, and rock stars seemed to be the main categories. I was told that the British society magazine *Tatler* had solemnly pronounced that this was the third most important social occasion of 2003. Then again, Elton John's birthday party was apparently number one in the same article, so it was a peculiar ranking system, to say the least.

Before this trip I hadn't even realized white tie existed. Now I knew it was one stage beyond black tie. Definitely not a surfing shorts and thongs occasion. The combination of the marvelously ornate palace with the hundred or so immaculately and formally dressed guests was quite breathtaking. Getting off our gondola at the entrance was ever so slightly like arriving at the Oscars—it felt grand and somehow important.

I, on the other hand, felt ill at ease and awkward. It wasn't just the prospect of yet another social engagement without drinking, but the fact that it was all but impossible to find any common ground. The first person I was introduced to, when she heard I was from Australia, said, "I simply love Australia. In fact, so much so that I wanted to move there, but my accountant tells me they don't do offshore." The second person, for some reason assuming I was a banker working in New York, told me she wasn't going to the Hamptons that year because it was getting too down-market. The third person told me her husband hadn't seen the inside of a commercial plane until he was twenty-one. Excellent, I thought, at last something I can engage with.

"What a shame," I said. "It must have been wonderful when he finally got the chance to travel."

She looked at me as if I was speaking Klingon before replying, "A *commercial* plane. Jimmy visited over seventy countries on his father's jet before he was eighteen." And so it went on.

It was these people—and a whole lot more like them—to whom I had to give a speech after dinner. We were clearly from parallel universes. They probably won't even understand me, let alone find me funny, I thought as I sat down to dinner. The guests at my table only increased my sense of "otherness." On either side of me were models. One of the "super" variety, the other of the "lingerie" variety. Kate was sitting at the head table in her capacity as matron of honor so I was left alone to tap-dance through the thoroughly alien (to me, anyway) *Tatler* crowd.

The first course arrived and the model on my left (lingerie) took one extremely small bite from it, wrinkled her nose, and then immediately put her knife and fork down and pushed the plate away from her. I resisted the temptation to do a Grace and say, "I'll have it," instead observing, "Caviar isn't my favorite either." She looked at me as if I were E.T.

It was only when she did exactly the same thing with all six courses that I realized it wasn't that *this* food wasn't to her taste, it was that *food* wasn't to her taste. She obviously didn't eat. At all. Over the course of the evening I swear she couldn't have had more than a dessertspoonful of food. In total. Then again, I bet she looked pretty acceptable in her lingerie. Bizarrely, the model (super) on my right ate like a horse the whole night. Thoroughly confusing.

The time for speeches came around all too quickly. Three of the groom's friends spoke before me, and their speeches were genuinely touching. Rather than a mindless rich kid on the international playboy circuit, Max clearly was a rather special guy who had earned the respect of everyone who had dealt with him through his hard work, humility, and decency.

Finally the microphone was handed to me. I was crapping myself as I stood up and the sea of beautiful faces turned my way. I'd not had so much attention focused on me since Kindi Gym. Except this time I was dying of nerves, not embarrassment. I couldn't have read my notes if I'd wanted to as I was half-blinded by the bling from all their jewelery, so I did what any self-respecting envious Brit does when he is out of his depth—I roasted Max. To my astonishment, they loved it, so I laid it on as thick as I could to ever-greater applause. Max took it in good spirit. The whole thing reminded me of the guy whom Burt Lancaster hires in *Local Hero* to tell him he's an idiot once a week, just to keep him honest.

With the speech out of the way I could relax, but unlike at the wedding in France, there wasn't a rugby match to sneak off to. Instead I made my way to the balcony with Kate and gazed at the incredible view. The dinner was being held in the Palazzo Pisani Moretta and the scene below of the Grand Canal and all its evening traffic was almost as good as the view of Cézanne's mountain from our room in Trets the week before.

I suddenly felt enormously fortunate. And then guilty about having had so many ungenerous and mean-spirited thoughts about the guests. Who the hell was I to be so censorious? The people back inside were human like the rest of us. It was a tribe thing. We all like to belong, and I didn't belong in their tribe. That doesn't make them any worse or me any better. Just because they didn't have money worries didn't mean they didn't have problems to deal with like everyone else. Just because I didn't have any common ground with them didn't make them in any way silly or superficial. I may not have had their specific financial or social advantages but in a different way I was every bit as spoiled as them. I resolved to go back inside and mingle "without prejudice," as George Michael almost said.

I turned to Kate. "You know, sweetheart, just because they've got money it doesn't mean that they are any happier," I told her.

"Course it does, you silly jerk," she replied. "Have you been drinking?"

Chapter 35

Mommy's Painting

THE DAY OF THE wedding started in glorious fashion. I was still
determined to keep up my training for the ocean swim. Luckily,
the rest of the wedding party had taken over the Hotel Cipriani
and as a wedding guest I had carte blanche to use all the hotel's
facilities—including its enormous heated outdoor pool.

I took the private launch to the island opposite St. Mark's
where the Cipriani is rather splendidly located, and made my way
to the pool area. Immediately upon arriving poolside, there was
a yell of "Nigel, Nigel, over here!" I looked around for the source
of such an embarrassingly loud and public invitation. On the
other side of the pool were three drop-dead gorgeous models I'd
met at dinner the night before. In their designer swimsuits, they
were frantically motioning to me while patting an empty chaise

longue next to them. I waved a pleasant hello and got on with my training as intended.

Actually that last sentence is a complete lie. What I really did was suck in my stomach as far as I could and swagger smugly across the terrace, hoping as many people as possible were noticing this demonstration of my physical magnetism to the opposite sex. The speech the night before had proved a minor hit and for one glorious hour I was an honorary member of their tribe.

Talk about beauty and the beast. I was wearing my surfing shorts and Saracens Rugby Club T-shirt. All three of them were in the smallest bikinis imaginable, had full makeup on, and were sporting elaborate hairdos. When I could hold my stomach in no longer, I got in the pool and showed off by doing a full thirty minutes of continuous front crawl. I was delighted with my swimming progress. The only downside of the training session was that by the time I got out I was once again a mere mortal. I obviously didn't look as good in the pool as I was starting to feel—the bevy of lovelies had long since left the poolside.

I got dressed quickly and hailed the private launch. I wanted to speak to the kids before the wedding ceremony. I called home immediately on my return to our villa.

"Hi, Liz, how are the kids doing?" I asked.

"They're fine. I'm sure they'd like to speak to you," she replied, passing the phone to Alex.

"Hi, Dad, was the *Bismarck* a warship?" he said.

"Yes, sweetheart. What've you been doing today?" I asked.

"Nothing. I've got a lollipop and I'm not afraid to use it."

"Er . . ."

"Dad, are weddings embarrassing?" he asked.

"Embarrassing, sweetheart?"

"Yeah. Liz told me you have to kiss someone in front of everyone," he explained.

Before I could think of a suitable reply, Eve grabbed the phone. "Sorry, Daddy, it wasn't on purpose. It was an accident. I was changing my mind up," she said.

"Don't explode, Dad, don't explode," Alex shouted in the background.

"Explode about what?" I asked. However, Eve had already passed the phone to Harry.

"Dad, I can count to a hundred," he said.

"Can you, darling? That is wonderful," I said, marveling at Liz's educational prowess, since he could barely count to ten when we left.

"Yeah, I'll show you. One, two, skip a few, three, four, skip some more, ninety-nine, one hundred. Eve drew on Mommy's painting," he added.

"Could I speak to Liz?" I asked. But the phone had been grabbed by Grace.

"Jingle bells, Batman smells. Where's Mommy? I want to talk to Mommy," she demanded.

"Mommy's not here at the moment, sweetheart, it's Daddy," I replied.

"Don't want to talk to you, I want Mommy," she answered.

My mind was reeling. Apart from the abuse and the confusion of this four-way conversation, I couldn't get "Mommy's painting" out of my mind. They were talking about one of our most prized possessions, a painting I had bought Kate for our previous wedding anniversary. More accurately, I had commissioned it. I had given the brief to a friend of ours, Mark Collis. My direction to him had been twofold and very specific.

"There are only two rules," I had told him. "One: It can't be of the bloody Opera House. Two: I do not want to know what it is until you are completely finished. You can paint a one-inch picture of a dog turd or a twenty-five-square-foot oil of Kate at the altar. The subject, medium, and size are entirely up to you. Regardless of whether we like it or not, I will buy it on the condition that neither of us finds out in advance what it is."

After nine weeks of painting, he unveiled it to us. Kate and I were both dumbstruck. He had painted an enormous exact copy of the two pages of the street map showing where we lived in Sydney. It covered the boys' school, the girls' preschool, the beach, the route of the ocean swim I was to do, the field where Alex plays rugby, the pitch where Harry plays football—everything. In one fell swoop he had captured our lives and provided us with a symbol of our Australian adventure. We absolutely adored it and now I had visions of it covered with scribbles.

Eventually I got Grace to stop telling me she loved Mommy more than me and she passed the phone to Liz, who confirmed that Eve had indeed shown great initiative, stood on a chair, and defaced our favorite painting.

"It was with washable paint, though, so I'm sure a good scrub will get it off," she optimistically informed me.

I was sure Mark hadn't painted with future Ajax scrubbings in mind, so I resigned myself to the fact that our favorite piece was ruined. How the hell was I going to break the news to Kate? With no job, commissioning artworks was going to be out of our reach for the foreseeable future, so I could hardly tell her I'd replace it as a sweetener. Beyond the painting itself, what on earth did this behavior say about how the kids were coping with our absence? A feeling of guilt and doubt came over me—regardless of what fun we were having. Perhaps it hadn't been such a bright idea after all to go off jaunting around Europe without the kids.

In the circumstances I thought my "Serbelloni selective honesty" policy was the best approach when I met up with Kate later that afternoon and she asked me how her angels were.

"Wonderful. They're all fine. Grace especially sends all her love. And Eve is learning to paint," I replied.

Chapter 36

Hearing Aid

RUINED FAMILY HEIRLOOM or not, it was now time to focus on the main event. We had the bride and her family staying with us, so there was a considerable amount of preparation involved. The villa was soon in a frenzy of well-ordered chaos. The place was crawling, not just with people getting dressed but also with yet more people *helping* those people get dressed. A handsome guy in jeans and a T-shirt whom I'd never seen before approached me.

"Are you all right if I do your hair now?" he inquired.

"What do you want to do with it?" I replied.

"Just to do it," he answered confusingly.

"Er, all right then."

I'd never had my hair "done" before. I haven't got that much of it to do. I keep it short, and a swift left-hand run-through in the morning has always seemed to do the trick. That said, it was strangely enjoyable to have someone fussing over it with such obvious concentration and seriousness. Fifteen minutes later, he held a mirror in front of me. To my mind, I looked like a cross between Elvis Presley and Don King. I went in search of Kate to ask how best to change it without causing offense. But within two minutes enough people had spontaneously commented on how great it looked for me to leave it how it was. Maybe the left-hand-through-the-hair strategy wasn't "leveraging the full potential of my best natural asset," as the hairdresser put it. Talk about different worlds.

The wedding service was held in one of Venice's landmark churches—the Basilica di San Giovanni e Paolo. The guests arrived in a flotilla of old wooden water taxis. It is against Venetian law to close such an icon for a private service, so the happy couple were wed in front of two hundred family and friends—and two hundred German, Japanese, and American tourists. To their credit none of them heckled or started the Mexican wave and it actually lent a slightly regal air to proceedings.

The trip to the reception intensified this feeling. As the flotilla of boats made its way down the Grand Canal and under the Rialto Bridge, the crowds that are ever-present in Venice started applauding, cheering, and waving. I felt like David Beckham must most days of his life. As in the pool earlier in the day, I gave in to my hidden shallows and rather than meekly blushing I started waving back. The adulation might have been unearned and totally misdirected but, damn, it felt good.

The reception was in the Cipriani Hotel. No expense or effort had been spared, and it was a wonderful evening. My enjoyment of events was further enhanced by the attentions of a gorgeous-looking middle-aged lady. By "attentions" I mean the full hand-on-forearm-leaning-right-into-my-personal-space-hanging-off-my-every-word-full-eye-contact type of attentions. I've always thought that the older Helen Mirrens and Isabella Rossellinis of this world give the younger Kate Mosses and Cindy Crawfords a damn good run for their money. Now I had one sitting next to me and she was making it painfully clear she was mine for the asking. If Kate had been looking she most definitely would have been able to tell that this woman was single. She wasn't so much interested as swooning.

I started to suspect I might be in luck when the first thing she did was—without any shame or embarrassment—move her chair unusually close to mine. My suspicions were further alerted when she announced, "My name's Sam. It's a lovely treat at my age to be sitting next to such a handsome younger man." She said this while all the time looking directly into my eyes and holding my hand and—I swear I'm not making this up—pulling me even closer. On several occasions she asked me to retell a story and laughed uproariously each time. Throughout the evening, when I was talking to her she would often mouth the words along with me as if I was some sort of guru imparting spiritual wisdom. On one bizarre occasion she even went so far as to ask me what men of my age found attractive in women. On another she made me repeat the name of the villa where we were staying three times. I don't want to brag, but it was clearly game, set, and match to the not-so-fat anymore, fired forty-year-old.

As Kate and I got ready for bed later that evening I couldn't resist retelling the story.

"I almost scored tonight, sweetheart." I graciously kicked off the conversation.

"Really," Kate replied, "and who was that with?"

"That good-looking middle-aged elegant woman, Sam something."

"And what precisely made you think she was flirting with you?"

"God, it was so obvious, it was embarrassing. She was clearly gagging for it. Whenever I was talking she would sort of lean in and look me in the face really intensely."

"Did she also cock her head slightly to one side at the same time?"

"Now you mention it—yes, she did. Quite endearing, really."

"And you say she leaned in when you were talking?"

"Yes—for God's sake woman, enough of this background context. I'm just trying to inform you that your husband is so magnetically attractive that he has to beat women off with a stick and tonight in particular I had a babe positively throwing herself at me."

"Okay, but one question. What does the fact that she leaned in closely when you were talking, and looked . . ."

"Gazed," I interrupted.

"Okay, *gazed* intensely at your face, say to you?"

"I've already told you—that she fancied me like mad. What the bloody hell does it say to you?"

"That she is Sam McClusker, one of my mother's oldest friends, who is completely deaf in one ear and extremely hard of hearing in the other. She lip-reads on formal occasions so she doesn't have to wear her hearing aid."

"Er . . . but she put her hand on my arm."

"Nigel, she has lived with her same-sex partner for eleven years. It's more likely that you'll get a job in the next month than that she would fancy you."

Women can be so unnecessarily cruel.

Chapter 37

Beaten Teachable

WE HAD PLANNED TO stay on in Venice for a few days after the wedding party left. This seemed like a good idea when we were booking the holidays, but in reality, with me not having a job and Venice being one of the most expensive cities in Europe, it meant moving to a small, overexpensive chicken coop of a tourist hotel. The free pass to the Cipriani's pool was no longer valid, either, so the swimming training was going to have to be put on hold until our return to Australia. It all served to heighten the vast chasm between the worlds of the ultrarich and the average tourist. There is no comparison. You can be in the same city, in the same street and still inhabit entirely parallel universes. There is nothing inherently wrong with either universe, it's just not perhaps such a good idea to juxtapose them as dramatically as we did.

Our new hotel room reminded me of one of those bottles with ships in them. I had no idea how they had got the tiny double bed into the room. You couldn't open the door more than a couple of feet before it hit the mattress. You then had to close the door before you could walk into the rest of the room. I say "walk into" but "edge around" is a more accurate description, as there were no more than ten inches between the bed and the wall. And that was it. No bathroom, no minibar, one cupboard that you couldn't open properly because of the bed, and a TV that didn't work fixed to the wall. It did for hotel accommodation what traveling on frequent-flyer miles does for airline travel. The location, however, was fantastic. We put our luggage on the bed (there was no other place for it) and headed out for a cheap dinner.

Venice doesn't really do "cheap dinner," so we ended up in a pizzeria. You'd be forgiven—but wrong—for thinking that a pizzeria so narrowed Kate's options that the ordering process was painless. If anything, it made it worse. After our traditional argument and sulk we settled down to one of those gorgeous evenings you sometimes have at the end of a successful and eventful vacation. We started by talking about the trip that we were on and relived every memorable moment. I fessed up to the real nature of my telephone conversations with the kids, and we laughed until people started to give us pointed looks.

We then moved on to *every* vacation we had been on together. We'd never actually taken this particular trip down memory lane before. Kate asked the waiter for a pen and we wrote them all down, first randomly, then again in chronological order. It was a strangely moving, intimate, and enjoyable process to go through.

It had been an incredible ten years. I was amazingly lucky. I was happy. I was relaxed. I felt like a drink.

"I think I'll have a glass of wine tonight, darling," I said.

"Don't be an idiot, Nigel," Kate said.

"No, seriously. Just one. I really feel like it. No beer or cocktails or anything like that. Just a single glass of an earthy, heavy red," I replied.

"What could possibly make you want to do something so ridiculously stupid?" Kate asked.

"Calm down, sweetheart. I'm only talking about one. I'm determined not to touch a drop when we get back to Australia. I just want a glass tonight. We don't have to get up early tomorrow. I'm feeling really happy. I'd like to drink something other than bloody mineral water tonight. Besides, all those vacation stories remind me of how much fun we used to have when we'd get it on together. It's been a great vacation, a real second honeymoon, and it seems a shame not to have at least one drink with you," I reasoned.

"So you've stayed dry in London, on the road trip, and at the two weddings, but now you want to 'crown a moment' in a crappy pizzeria? I don't know what they talk about in AA but it sounds to me like you're in denial."

"Jesus, I'm only talking about one. I feel I've earned it," I replied.

"Darling, you know it won't *be* one. You always say that but then one inevitably means another and then another."

"Well, all right, but it wouldn't really do any harm if we shared a bottle between us. Like we always used to do in the old days, just once more?" I suggested as I motioned to the waiter.

"Nigel, you've done so well," Kate said. "I'm really proud of you. Really proud. You've been a different man to live with. You're helpful. You're good with the kids. I can't believe you'd throw it all away. This is how it always starts. You feel you've proved you can control it by abstaining for a number of weeks, then you think you can go back to it in a moderate way. You can't. You spent ten years trying. You always failed. You'll be fine tonight. You'll probably be fine for a week, but I know in a month you'll be drinking more than you want to and then you'll be back to square one."

I felt my contradictory nature start to assert itself. Who the hell was she to tell me what to do? I didn't try and stop her from enjoying herself, so what gave her the right to try and stop me? She was such a killjoy. It was all right for her, sitting there with a cigarette and a cocktail, but what about me? Normally at this stage I would say something horrible to her and then to prove a point do exactly the opposite of what she wanted me to. The waiter approached.

"I'll have a latte, please," I heard myself say.

"I thought you wanted a drink," Kate said.

"I know. I did. But I don't. Well, I do but I don't—not when I think about it. You're right. I love you. I'm a stupid idiot. The whole point is never to pick up the first drink. Ever. I'm sorry," I said.

"Don't be. It's an amazing thing you've done. I just don't want you to go back. Not just for my and the kids' sakes, but for you. Having said that, if this was all some sort of elaborate ruse to say nice things to me to get my knickers off, you'll have to do better than that."

On reflection, it was one of the most important evenings of our entire marriage. I genuinely think Kate saved my life in that conversation. Or at the least saved me and the family from another ten years of failed moderate drinking. But it wasn't just an important evening in my life, it was also a revealing one.

After my moment of weakness had passed, Kate and I settled into a rather lovely flirty coziness during which I quizzed her on her seemingly natural ability to control her drinking.

"You never get wrecked or even drink more than you want to. You're always leaving drinks unfinished. I suppose we're just made up differently," I said.

"Maybe. But then again, what was that phrase they use in AA—'beaten teachable'?"

"Yep, that's it."

"Well, I think I wasn't so much beaten teachable as 'embarrassed sensible,'" she said.

"What do you mean?"

"Really want to know?"

"What do you think? Of course. Tell me."

"I've never told anyone this story before," she said.

"Get on with it—you're driving me to drink," I replied.

"You know the first job I had?"

"With the bank?"

"That's the one. It was all rather overwhelming. I was young . . ."

"Yeah, yeah. Enough of the excuses. Get on with it," I interrupted.

"Well, at the end of my first week one of the traders invited me to lunch. I was very flattered. I was just a secretary and he was one of the 'Masters of the Universe,' as Tom Wolfe called them."

"I get the picture: He wanted to nail you."

"Nigel."

"Sorry."

"Anyway, lunch was in a wine bar—this was the eighties, after all. I thought it was going to be just the two of us but there was a group of them. Men and women. They were all drinking champagne. Like it was water. They kept filling my glass. I was nervous, but enjoying it. It seemed so glamorous. The guys were all good-looking and every single one of them was flirting with me. Trouble was, I wasn't used to drinking so much—definitely not at lunchtime and definitely not champagne. After an hour we still hadn't ordered any food and I suddenly began to feel incredibly ill. I slipped off to the ladies' room and was violently sick."

"Silly, but nothing special," I said, unimpressed.

"Thing was, I didn't quite make the toilet. I got to the ladies' room but not to the stall. The moment I opened the door I was sick over the sink, floor, mirrors—the lot. It was like that scene from *The Exorcist*," Kate continued.

"What did you do?" I asked, horrified.

"It was hideous. The place was a real mess. I was desperate to impress my new colleagues so I tidied myself up as best I could and went back to the table they were all standing around."

"Leaving the restroom as it was?"

"Didn't really have much choice, I wasn't carrying a bucket and mop with me. I obviously needed to cover my tracks as I didn't want anyone to know it was me, so on my return I said in a loud voice, 'People can be so revolting: It's disgusting in the ladies' room, someone has been sick all over the room and just left it there.' I had all their attention and was going to continue but I was overcome with a second wave of nausea. Before I could even put my hand over my mouth I projectile-vomited onto the chest-high table we were gathered around. Christ, Nigel, it went everywhere. I don't think there was a person who wasn't hit. It was awful. Like when Eve was sick on the taxi driver on the way to Heathrow—times ten."

"I grant you, that is bad. What happened?"

"Everyone left to get cleaned up—it's not much fun eating lunch smelling of puke. I went home alone. Worst weekend of my life."

"And on Monday?" I asked.

"Everyone was really nice. Which bizarrely made it worse. The guy who had invited me called to say it didn't matter at all," Kate said.

"And did you see him again?"

"Course not. Neither he, nor indeed any of them, ever spoke to me again. The next Monday my boss called me in and let me go."

Chapter 38

Poo-poo Head

WHEN IT WAS FINALLY time to leave Venice there was no nice man to shepherd us to his boat to take us to the airport. We lugged our bags on public transport to the check-in desk of CrapAirlines. com and bid farewell to Venice from the microscopically small seats of our hundred-year-old 767. We were flying to London first, as the only flight to Sydney we could get was from Heathrow. We stayed in the country just long enough to drive from Stansted Airport to Heathrow, but it was still long enough for me to pick up the worst bout of hay fever that I'd had in years.

I have always been a chronic sufferer, and yet another of the benefits of Australia was that I hadn't had any symptoms at all since my arrival. I've long since learned to live with the effects of my allergy but this time my continual sneezing brought with it a whole new set of challenges. We were still in the height of the SARS scare and, as you can imagine, my sneezing made it a barrel of laughs disembarking and boarding during our stopover in Hong Kong. I had more fun with the community nurse.

When the plane started its descent into Sydney I was surprised at my emotions. I'd thought a three-week dose of the Northern Hemisphere would have made me homesick for England when in fact the reverse was the case. Sydney felt like home even though we hadn't even lived there for two years yet. Even something as simple as the surfboard bags on the baggage carousel made me smile and feel welcome.

However, although I love the city and was overjoyed to be "home," it doesn't mean that I was blind to its negative sides. For a start, we landed in driving rain. It's a bit like people not admitting that childbirth is actually extremely unpleasant, but there is a myth perpetuated about Sydney's weather. Take it from me: It does rain and it does get cold. It's entirely possible to have London weather for weeks at a time. When my parents first visited a year earlier it rained every day for a month.

This time, as soon as we passed through customs we were reminded of another of the less appealing aspects of the city. The taxis are without doubt the worst I've experienced anywhere in the world. It's not that they are dirty or dangerous or even unfriendly, it's just that the drivers haven't got a clue where they are going. Call me a stuffy old traditionalist, but I reckon that's a pretty core skill for a taxi driver. These guys don't even pretend.

"Bronte, please," I said as we climbed into the backseat.

"Where?"

"Bronte."

"Whereabouts?"

"Oh, about halfway down Macpherson Street, please."

"No, not whereabouts in Bronte. Where is Bronte?"

Now Bronte is possibly the second-most-well-known beach in Sydney. It's just a mile south of Bondi and barely four miles from the airport. It's a bit like a London cabbie not knowing where Hyde Park is, or Trafalgar Square.

"If you head toward Bondi, we'll show you the way," we offered.

"How do you get to Bondi?"

"Just head to the city center."

"Which way?"

I ended up getting out of the car and into the front passenger seat and directing him street by street. The thing is, this wasn't the first time this had happened to me. When I was working I had often been asked to direct cabbies for trips *within* the city center.

But not even a crappy Sydney taxi ride could spoil my mood as we approached the house. I was almost ill with excitement. I hadn't seen our kids for three whole weeks—the longest time ever. Alex was first to the door.

"Daddy, Daddy, the Saracens have signed Taine Randell!"

Harry was close behind. "Daddy, how does hair grow?"

Eve appeared. "Daddy, you've got grass on your face." (I'd grown a beard on the trip.)

Grace finally presented herself. As I opened my arms to give her a hug she walked up, looked me in the eye, and announced, "You're not my father, poo-poo head," before walking off.

Not sure whether the poo-poo head or doubted parentage jibe hurt more, but as I lugged our bags inside I couldn't help saying a silent prayer in hope that it was only Eve who had taken up painting in our absence.

Chapter 39

Pinch and a Punch

OUR EUROPE TRIP PROVED to be a real watershed. Slipping back into domestic life felt good, comfortable. I got stuck into the kids' lives as never before. School cafeteria became a regular duty; I even coached the under-six football team on occasions. The latter is more difficult than it sounds. The phrase "herding cats" springs to mind. The angelic little bastards just wouldn't listen. As I was talking, they'd all be gazing off into the distance or scratching their nuts or fighting. I found it a totally draining experience. The next week I watched the regular coach do it with none of the problems I had encountered. Afterward I asked him how he did it.

"The secret is to keep them moving," he explained. "If you get them to do things, they are fine. The moment you ask them to stand still and listen to you, it's carnage."

I thought back to the week before. He was right. Amazing how something so simple could make such a difference. I realized that over the months off I had been picking up tips like this one on a weekly basis. All of them were making me a more capable father—not to mention a happier one. These tips regularly made the difference between me having a shitty day or a wonderful one.

I had, for example, come to hate school pick-up. Every day I had an argument with Alex—me wanting him to come home right away, him wanting to stay and play football. It was ruining the end of each day for the family. I would arrive home furious and Alex would sulk. This in turn would make Kate upset. Not the ideal combination for arsenic hour. Then one day I asked a friend how he seemed to manage it so well.

"You really want to know?" he inquired.

"Yes."

"Okay. Why are you so keen to take him home right after the bell has rung?"

The question threw me a bit. I had no idea, it was just what you did, wasn't it? School pick-up was a task that I was volunteering to do, and in a typically male fashion I had decided that like all tasks it needed to be done quickly and efficiently. I explained this to my adviser.

"Okay, I understand, but if you let him play for fifteen minutes and then took him home what would happen?"

"What do you mean, 'happen'?"

"I mean, what would be bad about it?"

I thought for a moment. "Nothing," I replied.

"Okay. What would happen it you let him play for half an hour and then took him home?"

"Nothing."

"Okay then. What would happen if you let him know in advance that you were always going to let him have thirty minutes of playing after school before you took him home?"

"We'd never have an argument, he'd have more time with his friends playing outdoors as opposed to watching TV, I wouldn't lose my temper, and the evenings at home would be infinitely more pleasant."

"I'd recommend you try it then," he suggested.

I pondered his advice. "There's a flaw," I eventually said.

"What?"

"Well, what if I don't want to spend half an hour each day hanging around a kids' playground?" I asked.

"Then you don't. You're thinking about this all wrong. It's not supposed to be a military operation with a medal for who can do things quickest. Watch your son, get to know his friends, chat to the other dads and moms. If you don't want to do that, then use the time to make calls on your mobile. Lastly, if you really can't spare the time, turn up at three twenty-five, not three o'clock."

"Is that allowed?"

"Of course it is."

"Do you do it?"

"All the time. As long as you let him know, he'll be fine with it. My lad prefers it."

After this conversation I actually looked forward to school pick-up as one of my favorite bits of the day. There were countless examples like this. None of them were splitting the atom—indeed some of them were as simple as leaving the butter out of the fridge overnight so making packed lunches in the morning was easier—but they all contributed to transforming my days.

It made me think back to when I was working and how on many occasions I was too busy doing things badly to ask for, and then listen to, advice. I resolved that if I ever went back to work, I would remember this simple lesson: If you are regularly struggling with a task, try asking the counsel of someone who excels at the thing you are struggling with. The worst that can happen is that they refuse—although this has never happened in my time off and I somehow think it wouldn't in the workplace, either. People on the whole are delighted to be asked about things they're good at.

Rather astonishingly, given the outcomes of my first attempts, I even started to enjoy taking the kids to school in the mornings. I actually preferred it when I could take all four of them in the car together—dropping the girls off at preschool first, then driving on to school with the lads. Seeing the girls with their pink and blue lunch bags on their backs walk hand in hand into the building was as cute as the conversation in the car with the boys was funny.

"Lads, that's a revolting smell. Which one of you monsters has farted?" I asked one morning as I got back into the car having kissed the twins good-bye.

"Not me, Dad, it was Alex," Harry said.

"He who denied it supplied it: It was Harry," Alex countered.

"He who smelt it dealt it: It was you, Dad." Harry changed tack.

"He who rhymed it crimed it: You're both guilty. Besides, you know Dad doesn't fart," I replied.

"Daaaad," they both chorused.

It was puerile but fun. I was finding that I could get the most enormous amounts of joy out of the simplest of things. Harry would stand next to me in the mornings and mimic me shaving. The girls would lie on either side of me when I was doing sit-ups and raise their arms and legs while shouting, "Look at us, Mommy. We're exercising." Alex and I would sit on the same armchair together and watch *The Simpsons* most evenings—all the time with him impersonating the characters and making unflattering comparisons between Homer and me.

The beginning of each month was a particular favorite. Far too early in the morning, all four of them would burst into our bedroom and pummel me with a traditional "pinch and a punch for first of the month." I would just lie there moaning "white rabbits" while Kate would egg them on by saying, "Ignore him, too late." When I moved into the "slap and a kick for being so quick" mode of defense, Kate would simply change the rules, scream, "Get Daddy!" and join in on the kids' side. Women.

Chapter 40

Nelson Bay

IT WASN'T JUST THE family routine that I was increasingly happy with—I was also starting to get on top of my personal game. For the first time since I was nineteen, I was now at my ideal weight. It hadn't been easy but I had stumbled on a workable weight-loss regime (maybe I'll write that diet book after all), and I loved how it made me feel. The swimming training was also well on track. The week after our return from Europe I stuck to my plan of starting to train in the ocean.

To begin with, Clovelly, the next beach down from Bronte, was my choice as it has a long, thin stretch of water protected on three sides from the elements. The training had clearly paid off. I had expected it to be a bit of a shock when I switched from the pool to the sea but after the first few tries I found I wasn't bad at it—and, more important, I loved doing it.

Within a couple of weeks I was a regular at Clovelly and a convert to the whole ocean-swimming experience. Being indoors swimming between ropes in flat chlorinated water or outside in the confines of an ocean pool no longer seemed to be the real thing. I started to really look forward to each session. I found it impossible to be tired or miserable after even the shortest of swims in the sea, and the sights, sounds, and smells of the ocean soon came to be as important to me as the exercise itself.

After a few more weeks I was confident enough to start training with friends, mainly on the weekends. These friends were all qualified lifeguards and had done truckloads of proper ocean races. Swimming with them meant I could broaden my horizons beyond Clovelly and before too long I was swimming at all six beaches from Bondi down to Maroubra. I was touched that they would spare the time to mess around with such a novice as me.

It was with real pride that I did my first beach-to-beach swim. It was a rough day. I had decided to attempt the short distance across Nelson Bay from Tamarama around the headland to Bronte. For a local, this swim would seem like stepping over a small puddle; for me it was like swimming across the Pacific. I deliberately chose a rougher day to experience a bigger swell because an important part of the challenge of ocean races is getting in and getting out. The year before, fifteen people had to be rescued at Bondi during the Bondi to Bronte race, because getting out beyond the breaking surf was too demanding. Swimming in a pool is tiring, but getting out through substantial breaking waves is a different challenge altogether. As a beginner, if you get it wrong the chances of you being able to swim another two miles in open sea are dramatically reduced.

As with the school run, I decided to ask for advice. My friend David, who had given me the slow-and-steady swimming tip earlier in the year, kindly agreed to help. He was an excellent coach.

"The important thing is to dive well before the wave reaches you," he said. "Swim deep, grab sand if you can. Stay down and swim at least a couple of strokes after you feel the wave pass over you before you come up. You don't want to come up in the backwash froth, as that is seriously debilitating if you do it a couple of times. When you come up, be prepared to immediately dive again. It is tiring but under no circumstances stop until you are out beyond the surf. If you do, you'll just end up being caught in the washing machine where all the waves dump. That's a dangerous place to be—even for a good swimmer."

It was clear from the way David said this that in his eyes I didn't qualify for that particular description. It was all a little bit daunting as I stood there watching the waves roll in. I thought to myself, *What on earth am I playing at? I'm a pudgy, unfit businessman who doesn't really have the right to be in swimming trunks, let alone to be on this beach about to do this swim. But then again, screw it. That is why I'm here—precisely because I don't want to be a pudgy, unfit businessman.*

Clinging to this last motivational thought, I walked into the water and promptly got knocked off my feet. David helped me up and shouted in my ear, "*After* the last wave of this set, I want you to follow me." Two more waves broke before he made his move. I followed him as if my life depended on it. Come to think of it, it probably did. I can well imagine how rooted you would be if you got caught in the middle of the breaking waves and had expended all your energy—there is only so much a lifeguard can do. I now properly understood how there could still be so many fatalities each year.

I followed David's instructions to the letter and within a few exhausting minutes I was successfully beyond the breakers. It was wonderful. I loved the feeling of the swell as it repeatedly picked me up and brought me down again. It was the first time I had ever been properly "in the ocean," as opposed to "at the beach." I floated on my back for a while looking at Tamarama beach in front of me, Bondi beach to my right, and Bronte to my left. For some reason I couldn't help laughing.

At the risk of getting religious, it was as near to a numinous experience as any I'd had recently—and that includes in the Quaker house. We had to swim farther out to avoid the riptide off the north Bronte headland. The farther the better, as far as I was concerned—I didn't want the swim to end. A surprise, and a real bonus, was that even though we were what seemed like miles off the shore, I could see the bottom, and all the glorious sea life in between, the whole way around.

As we made our way toward the south end of Bronte beach we passed behind a group of surfers that the big wave conditions had attracted. A year earlier, if I had been standing on this beach on a day like this I wouldn't have been able to imagine being in the sea, let alone being as far out as the surfers. Now I was passing behind them. Despite the few mouthfuls of water I had inadvertently swallowed on the journey, I felt like a cross between Jacques Cousteau and Johnny Weissmuller when I climbed onto dry land at the Bronte beach pool.

For David it had been a quick dip in the sea; for me it was a huge milestone, a real rite of passage. As we stood chatting, I became aware of another remarkable aspect of what we'd just done. Not the swim itself, but the fact that it was winter and we'd both just swum across Nelson Bay without the need for wet suits or caps. Have I mentioned that I love Australia?

Chapter 41

Blue Line

IT WAS AS IF THE benefits of being off the treadmill were not only cumulative but exponential as well. Five months into my year off, it all seemed to be coming together. I'd never been happier. Another source of joy was that on top of all the swimming I was doing I had also made a successful return to my running career.

I first took up running on January 1, 1996, and have kept a diary of every run I have done ever since. To date I've filled three books cover to cover with small, densely packed writing. Reviewing them gives a sort of arm's-length commentary on my life. All my travels are detailed, because wherever I go I always take my running shoes. I don't believe I've really experienced a city unless I've run in it. I "collect" cities and look forward to each new one so I can tick it off on the map.

Sometimes my runs are what I remember most fondly of a visit. A run around the Imperial Palace was the highlight of a trip to Tokyo; same with a jog around Central Park last time I was in New York. In 1997, I went to Athens on a horrendous business trip where I was expected to visit nightclubs and brothels with a client—"eating and drinking for other people's pleasure," as the famous business commentator Sir Harvey Jones so wonderfully described business entertaining.

The run I did up Lykavittos Hill made the trip for me, although refusing to partake of the delights on sale in the Moscow Queens strip club did nothing for my reputation with the client. I don't just collect cities on my runs, I collect people too—friends, work colleagues, family, strangers; anyone and everyone I've run with has in some way enriched me, and they get recorded in the diary.

Running is a fantastic leveler and an excellent way to get to know someone a little more deeply than you normally would. Gender, seniority, and age become somehow irrelevant when you're two miles into a jog around Sydney Harbor. (I find that surfing, or indeed anything that involves taking your shirt off, can potentially have the same beneficial effect.)

Most important, in the past running had transformed my relationships with my children. When my elder son turned one, I reviewed my parental performance and concluded I was a lousy dad. Nothing too bad, just not really properly involved. I went out that day and bought one of those baby jogger strollers. I then told Kate that on Saturday mornings she was banned from doing anything with Alex.

From that day on I got up every Saturday and took Alex for a run to somewhere he found interesting—usually a train station, for the first eighteen months. We'd sit there chatting and when he got bored I'd run back. He got out of the house, Kate got a break, and I got a bonding opportunity with my son as well as some exercise. It worked so well that I did the same with Harry, and when Grace and Eve were born I went out and bought a double stroller and did the same with them. When they are older they will probably tell their friends that the worst bit of their childhood was the bloody runs they had to do with their dad, but for me they're some of my most special memories.

For the years until we came to Australia, I was running three times a week, on average, but since the move, the pressures of the job and four kids had taken their toll to such an extent that whole months had passed without me so much as lacing a sneaker. To most people, that would be no great loss but for me it bordered on the tragic. I loved running. It had become a central part of my life and was responsible for many of its high spots.

I'm well aware that my relationship with the "sport" is alternative to say the least. I don't view it as a physical activity: I view as a spiritual one. Many casual joggers speak of how they feel their running not only keeps them fit but also gives them self-confidence and heightens their appreciation of the world they live in. I too can attest to these feelings—but for me running does more than that. In many ways I credit it with saving my life. I genuinely believe my running has made me not just a better father and husband, but a better person period.

One of my cornerstone philosophies is that with sustained, focused effort, you can achieve almost anything. Now, as a theory on its own this can come across as a bit Pollyannaish, but every time I run, I can reinvent myself how I want to be. Every race I finish, every person I connect with, and every city I discover proves my life philosophy back to me.

Running also keeps me honest. In 1996 I resolved to run at least one race a year. The clock doesn't lie or listen to excuses—if the newspaper says you did the 10K in seventy minutes, then you did. It doesn't mention that you were really stressed at work and couldn't find the time away from the family to train. It just says you ran the 10K in seventy minutes. It's truth stripped down to its barest form.

Whether you think running ten kilometers in seventy minutes is pathetic or heroic is your business. It just is. It provides you with a rock of certainty in an otherwise rather confusing world. What you do with that truth is up to you. The glorious thing is if you do decide to improve it, the results of your efforts are laid bare in the same manner. Unlike so many things in life, you can't fake it: You either improved or you didn't.

When I was in London my regular race was the Crouch End 10K. I did the first one alone. I was starting out and running was personal, almost a guilty secret. However, each year after that, I made a point of running with friends and family and having a party in our house afterward. In 1998 I ran it with my brother, my sister-in-law, my brother-in-law, my sister-in-law's boyfriend, Giles, and three work colleagues. Both Kate's parents and mine, plus an assortment of friends from the area, came to the postrace lunch in our kitchen.

I have a picture taken in the garden on that day. When they are writing my obituary I'd be very happy for it to be the one they use. If only every family or social occasion was so stress-free and joyful. Think large family Christmas without the bickering. I've still got my finisher's T-shirt from each of the six Crouch End 10Ks I've done, and nerdy as it is, they would be the first clothes I'd rescue if the house caught fire.

To avoid injury after such a long layoff I had deliberately got back in to my running slowly. I actually started with a series of short walks, gradually extending the route each time. When I got up to a full thirty minutes I tentatively added in short bursts of jogging between random markers that I would set on the spur of the moment. "Right, you fat tub of lard, let's see if you can jog to that bus stop from here," I'd challenge myself before running to this self-imposed finish line and continuing to walk again.

To my slight surprise and delight, within a couple of months I was injury-free and back to a regular running schedule. In fact my running was going well (and by "well" I most definitely don't mean fast or long—I mean enjoyable). A surfing instructor once said to me the best surfer is the one who is smiling the most. By applying that criterion to running, I was comfortably more successful than Carl Lewis and Linford Christie put together, so I signed up for the City to Surf race with my friend Sally.

This is an amazing event. It starts in the center of the city, in Hyde Park, and as the name suggests makes its way to the surfing beach at Bondi. Fourteen kilometers in all, it is the world's biggest timed running event with over sixty thousand runners participating each year.

Sydney seems to have a knack for doing these types of occasions incredibly well. Throughout the year there are numerous community events—not just sporting festivals, but everything across a spectrum as diverse as Gay Mardi Gras, the New Year's Eve fireworks, and Sculpture by the Sea. People turn up to these happenings in the thousands and the events always seem to be immaculately run and trouble-free. No wonder the Sydney Olympics were such a success.

On the sunny morning in August, it was wonderful just waiting in the crowd at the starting line. Sixty thousand people, all in a good mood, gathered for a common purpose. My strongest memory of the day is the surreal image of the sky filled with flying clothes as people threw their prerace sweatshirts into the trees just before the starter's gun. It was like those scenes in *Lord of the Rings* when the archers all fire their crossbows into the air at once, except here it was shirts, not arrows. By the time the gun went off, every tree was dressed like an alternative Christmas tree. This being Sydney, the organizers of course had a plan for this annual tradition and collected all the discarded tops for charity.

The race itself was a joy. I was determined not to get caught up in the macho "reach for the sky" bullshit that can sometimes overtake you on race day. My race plan was to start out slow, get slower, then taper off toward the end. I wanted to savor every minute. A bit like my Nelson Bay swim, the longer I took the better, as far as I was concerned. I'm pleased to report I excelled myself in this regard, coming in 33,748th place behind an assortment of runners dressed as nuns, elephants, and one nutcase who I swear was wearing a full diving suit and hood. Despite my distance behind the lead runner, this race ranks up there as one of my all-time favorites. The T-shirt I got from the event has pride of place in my wardrobe along with all the Crouch End 10K shirts.

I was so enthused by the City to Surf, and encouraged by how well the family was getting on with one another, that I decided to take the plunge and enter a race with both Alex and Kate for the first time. Luckily another of the finest fun runs on the planet— the Bridge Run—was only a month or so away. This route starts at the North Sydney Oval, winds its way gently across the Harbor Bridge (which is specially closed for the occasion), and ends at the Opera House. Oh, and the whole way you are running on the blue line that is still on the roads from the marathon course of the 2000 Olympic Games. Talk about collecting a city.

We sent off our entry forms and started the process of preparing for our first race together. Neither Alex nor Kate being runners, this was more of an operation than it might sound. At times coaxing them out the door in their training shoes reminded me of the persuasion I had to engage in to get Kate to do her bungee jump, but on the whole our jogs together were even-tempered affairs. Besides, however hard I may sometimes have had to push, at least there were never any gators involved.

Chapter 42

Jaws

ALL IN ALL IT WAS A pretty dramatic turnaround from the fat, lethargic executive I had been just a few months before. I loved being active and slim. I found myself in a virtuous circle of energy: The fitter I got, the more I wanted to do and so the fitter I got. I reached another swimming milestone—again with David. This time it was swimming from head to head, not beach to beach. We dived off the edge of the famous Icebergs pool on the south head of Bondi Bay and swam to the north head and back again—a decent distance even for a good swimmer. This may sound incredibly sad but I was so excited by the prospect of this challenge that I actually counted every single stroke I took: 2,200 exactly. As I climbed out of the ocean onto the edge of the Icebergs pool, I couldn't help thinking that Zane would have been impressed—even if I was still six hundred strokes short.

With this feat successfully behind me, I felt sufficiently in shape to apply for the Bondi to Bronte race. Up until then I hadn't felt I'd earned the right to even fill out the entry form. Reading the form, however, was an intimidating experience in its own right. One particular bit stood out from the rest, and I quote: "Please note the Bondi to Bronte ocean swim is a demanding event. Possible risks include drowning, being hit by a boat, shark attack, or bluebottle sting. Swimmers enter at their own risk and are responsible for their own physical condition." Sell it to me, why don't you.

One of the many benefits of my new state of fitness was that my surfing had gradually begun to improve. I'd been hooked from the very first lesson I'd taken on Christmas Day 2001, at Bondi, but my progress had been frustratingly slow. Unless you've grown up near the water, surfing is actually an incredibly difficult thing to do. To a beginner surfer, those videos of the guys riding monster waves in Hawaii are as relevant as videos of Tiger Woods winning the U.S. Open are to a novice golfer. It gives you no idea how difficult it is. To start with I'd found it a stretch to even carry the damn board along the beach, let alone paddle the thing in the ocean.

For a beginner, paddling out is exhausting. Just as you think you've got the hang of being on the board, a wave hits you, knocks you off, and sweeps you back toward the beach. There is no respite. The waves are relentless. You simply have to keep getting back on the board and paddling for all you're worth. The goal is to get out back behind the surf where you can sit up, have a rest, and read the ocean for the best place to catch the breaks. On many days it is impossible for novice surfers to make it out back. There is an unofficial safety code that says that if you can't get out back quickly then the conditions are too big for your standard and you should get the hell out of the water.

Like many things in life, surfing is completely unfair for the beginner. Just as banks only lend money to the people who don't need it, surfing becomes easier and more effortless the better you get. Paddling a surfboard uses muscles you don't use when sitting at a desk working on a computer. After my first lesson I ached for a week and winced every time I had to move my shoulders back to get a shirt or jacket on. The first time I made it out back I was so shattered that rather than sitting up and looking around, I lay facedown on the board like a beached whale and gently moaned.

But getting out back isn't the half of it. You then have to learn how to catch a wave. And leap to your feet. And ride a wave. This takes not only skill but also strength and agility.

Regular surfers have bodies that defy the normal rules of human evolution. Forget the ludicrous bodybuilder physique—these guys and gals have perfectly sculpted forms. Not an ounce of fat on them. Rock-hard muscle honed purely around the specific actions needed while on a surfboard. Broad shoulders, V-shaped backs, and entirely flat stomachs are the norm. Throw in the sun-bleached hair and year-round tans and you can see why surfer culture is seized upon by marketers as diverse as Coke and FCUK and is even used in countries that haven't actually got beaches.

Kate and I saw many such posters while in Venice and the French Alps. I suppose the skiing link could explain the posters in the Alps—but Venice? Unlike many supposedly inspirational looks that are obviously artificial and manufactured, the surfer dude has a certain rugged credibility about him that signals authenticity. It certainly appealed to me—but then again, as Kate regularly reminded me, I was clearly going through a midlife crisis.

I was now capable of getting out back in moderate conditions. Reading the ocean was my new problem—that and the surf code. A city beach such as Bondi is often crowded. Breaking the surf rules is a definite no-no, and being a beginner is no excuse. The main principle is that you never, ever, "drop in," which basically means that the person who catches the wave first has right of way. If you catch it later and drop in on a surfer who is already riding the wave, you piss them off mightily. Given their size, this is not something I recommend.

Getting out back brings with it another problem. Sharks. I've never been sure precisely where the shark net is at Bondi. On days when the tide is out and the surf is big you can find yourself way out to sea. It's only natural to start wondering. And rural beaches don't even have shark nets. Locals readily admit there are sharks in the ocean. They have a refreshingly simple, two-pronged safety policy: "If you are worried about sharks, either get out of the ocean or get over it."

To be fair to them, "getting over it" involves slightly more than just not worrying. There are certain basic rules that you are advised to follow to avoid being taken by a shark. One of them is not to surf at dusk or dawn, another is never surf alone. In my newfound enthusiasm I idiotically ignored both on a weekend trip to the aptly named Boomerang beach, a few hours north of Sydney.

I had woken early. The kids and Kate were still asleep. My surfboard was on the roof of the car from the journey the day before. It was calling to me. I could have a surf, buy breakfast for the family, and be back before they woke up, I self-servingly reasoned. I leaped out of bed, flung my clothes on, and drove the two miles to Boomerang beach.

After a while you tend to get blasé about beaches in Australia. It's a bit like going snow-blind while on a skiing holiday. There are so many nice beaches that you come to expect miles of white sand, clear water, and gorgeous views. Even by Australian standards, however, this one was a pretty nice beach and, wonderfully, it was completely deserted. Not a soul in sight. It was still semidark; the sun just starting to appear on the horizon. The waves were a decent size, but I got out back without any bother.

I sat up on the board and soaked in the moment. I was on vacation, in the ocean before breakfast. This was everything I had dreamed Australia would be. At times like these I ignored the fact that I was a forty-year-old unemployed ad executive and that I had no idea how the family was going to support itself. I couldn't be luckier, I thought to myself.

No sooner had I finished counting my blessings than a slate-gray flash in the water to my left caught my eye. Or was I imagining it? I had, after all, just been daydreaming. No, there it was again. I wondered what it was. I looked around. The beach was still deserted. Although it was foolhardy to be out here alone, I felt comfortable. The conditions were well within my capability. If I got tired I could easily paddle in within a few minutes. The only thing that could possibly go wrong was a shark attack, and how likely was that, for Christ's sake? I mean, they were incredibly rare, weren't they? There hadn't been a shark-related fatality since we'd moved to Oz. Well, there had been that diver who was killed, and that German tourist, but they were the exceptions.

Suddenly the *Jaws* panic gripped me. *For God's sake, Nigel,* I thought. *What are you playing at? I'm alone in the ocean before the break of dawn. If anything happened I'd be screwed. It wouldn't even need to eat me. Just a leg or an arm, a hand even, would do it. I'd never make it to shore—there's no one here to even try to rescue me. I'll just drown pathetically. Kate doesn't even know where I am. Snap out of it, calm down, take a few breaths, look around, get your bearings, then gently paddle to shore. I'm getting a bit chilly anyway.*

I felt better. A bit silly, in fact. I was always having these *Jaws* fantasies. Best to save the drama for when I was actually in one. I started paddling to shore. And stopped again as a fin, no farther than ten feet away, glided across the front of my board, between me and the beach.

That was a fin, it is a shark, I am screwed, I thought in quick succession.

I attempted to sit up with my feet on the board, and promptly fell off. You normally use your legs in the water for balance when you sit on a surfboard. I hadn't developed the skill of sitting on the board without them. Then again, I thought, I won't have any bloody legs if I don't get them out of the water pronto. I hauled myself onto my board and lay flat on it. One of the few advantages of being a beginner is that you have a bigger board. Mine was over eight feet long. I could lie on it with no part of me touching the water.

The fin appeared again, this time to my right. *Jesus, it's sizing me up for breakfast. Surely if I just lie here it will go away. I mean to shark's eyes, I must just look like an eight-foot bit of wood.* It was then I remembered an article in the weekend's paper about how sharks can detect human urine from over one hundred yards away. A marvelous memory, given I'd only recently indulged in one of the delights of an early morning surf—a warm piss into a cold wet suit.

This is quite serious, I thought. *I'm actually going to die. Talk about irony. I was just putting it all together and I'm bloody well going to be eaten by a bloody fish before I can enjoy it all. I wonder if Kate will remarry? Alex will probably captain the British Lions and I'll miss it because I'll be an unfound skeleton at the bottom of the sea off the New South Wales coast. At least I won't have to watch boys with all the wrong intentions taking my twins out. How will the family support itself? The life insurance will go some way to easing the first year, I suppose. Hang on—what life insurance? You're unemployed, you idiot, you haven't got any life insurance. Oh balls, I've really screwed it up this time.*

The fin appeared again, this time followed by another one and another. *Oh, shag me senseless in Bourke Street, they are hunting in a pack.* I gingerly got my car key out of the waterproof pocket in my ankle strap. *Great, I'm going to ward off three sharks with a Toyota key.*

It would be fair to say it was one of the low points of my year. Lying on a surfboard, surrounded by circling sharks, shivering with fear, and clutching a car key in self-defense. I looked to the beach. PEOPLE! I could definitely see people. Two of them. Carrying surfboards. Hold on, it looks like they are getting *in*. Shit, I should warn them. Can sharks hear? Hell, if I shout it could annoy them. Then again, maybe they will eat the other surfers, not me. Christ, they're paddling out this way. Jesus, they're coming to say hello. The fins were clearly visible, this time to my left again.

"How're you going," they said as they got out back next to me. "Isn't it great this morning?"

"BeachgotobeachgetoutofthewaterfinsthreefinsItriedto warnyou," I whispered incoherently.

"What's that, bro? Yeah, three of them. Bloody wonderful—surfing with dolphins before breakfast. Sets you up for the day, doesn't it? Is that a car key in your hand? You can get a pocket for those if you buy the right ankle strap," one said, before turning around to study the ocean swell.

Don't know about setting me up for the day, but the breakfast I took back to Kate and the kids sure as hell tasted good.

Chapter 43

Show and Tell

As WELL AS A chance to make permanent life changes like kicking the booze and getting fit, I also viewed my time off the corporate wheel as a once-in-a-lifetime opportunity to do some of the more minor, onetime things on my personal wish list—the sort of things people say they'd like to do but never get around to for whatever reason. One of these things was a Lads and Dads trip. Well, Lads and Dad, to be precise, as I wanted to do it alone.

Pressures of work and the realities of having four kids meant it was extremely rare for me to spend proper time just with my sons. Because Harry was still only five, I was forever going off with just Alex. Whether it is for this or other reasons, Alex and I had developed an incredibly strong bond.

I desperately wanted to do things with both of them, but below a certain age it is difficult. I had tried taking Harry with us to rugby games on a couple of occasions but he was too young and I ended up feeling guilty that I was forcing him to do something he clearly wasn't enjoying. I adored Harry with a passion and didn't want him to think there was any favoritism.

My suspicions that he wasn't convinced of this weren't so much aroused as rammed through my heart with a stake when I awoke one morning to find Harry standing by my side of our bed. As usual he had his pajamas on inside out and his hair was sticking up like a mad professor. I could have eaten him, he was so cute.

"Morning, Bonkers," I said.

"Morning, Daddy," he replied. "Daddy? Who do you love best? Alex or me?"

"Sweetheart! I love you all equally—you know I do," I exclaimed.

"Okay, Dad. Daddy, I can spell market. M-a-k-i-t," he said before wandering off.

Leaving the issue of his spelling aside, I was determined to use this little exchange as the spur to make me seize the moment and actually go on, as opposed to talk about, a Lads and Dad adventure.

As keen as I was to do a trip, I was equally keen not to replicate some of the mistakes my own parents made on similar outings. I have extremely strong memories of well-intentioned but disastrous family vacations where our parents assumed my brother and I would like the same things they did. A car trip around the New England forests particularly sticks in my mind.

Four days spent driving through trees. Trees. No girls. No rugby. Just trees. Mom and Dad were busily oohhing and aahhing at the "lovely views," while my brother and I were not so quietly going insane with the pointlessness of it all. After two hours, we ended up sitting on the floor of the car playing cards while Mom and Dad looked at the scenery for the next three and a half days. Sightseeing just isn't an activity for anyone under twenty. Especially "landscape sightseeing." Talking to my friends, I discovered all of them, without exception, have their own horror stories of vacations spent stuck in the backs of cars having to look at scenery.

My idea was to drive the lads to Canberra, stay a night, and drive back the next day. The location wasn't important. I just wanted to do a boys' trip. None of us had been to Canberra and it was the right distance away. Alex and Harry were ecstatic when I suggested it to them.

"Will we have KFC, Daddy?" Harry said.

"Does the hotel have a TV?" Alex asked.

"Yes and yes," I replied. I was determined not to force them to look at or do anything on this trip. I don't know if this qualifies me as a crappy dad, but given that we spent every other waking hour forcing them to do or not do stuff, I figured a day and a half off wouldn't do them any harm. They could spend the entire time eating KFC in the hotel room while watching TV as far as I was concerned, as long as we had a laugh together.

It was a blast from the moment we got in the car. At the first station, I stopped for gas and treats. I also bought a disposable camera. Alex had received a *Harry Potter* tape from his grandmother so they spent the two hours before our lunch stop munching candy; listening to Harry, Ron, and Hermione getting in and out of trouble; and never once looking out the window at the view. As it happens, the view is rather nice so I had a decent time as well.

Lunch was a dietician's nightmare—hamburgers, fries, ice cream, and candy for after. I read the *Goulburn Gazette* and nursed a latte. I was still off the booze and I couldn't help musing that I

wouldn't have been doing this trip if I weren't. Or worse: I would
be doing it but looking for every opportunity for a cleansing ale
and finding the kids irritating in the meantime. Goulburn's news
was hardly earth-shattering, but I found it strangely comforting
reading about the proposed pavement-widening scheme that had
local residents up in arms.

We strolled back to the car. As we were doing so, I felt a little
hand creep into mine. I glanced down and said, "Hi, Harry."
For once he didn't correct me on his name. Then, more surprisingly, I felt another hand creep into my other hand. This time it
was Alex. This didn't happen much anymore, now that he was
eight and there were usually schoolmates around who might see.
I deliberately took the long way back to the car so I could prolong
the walk with all three of us holding hands.

Another two hours of *Harry Potter* and we were approaching
the outskirts of Canberra. We drove past a big roadside poster for
Virgin Blue airline, simply headed: "Next time take the plane.
Sydney to Canberra $69 round-trip." It was obviously aimed
at the business audience, not the Lads and Dad target market.
However, for the first time in months it made me think about
the advertising business and how I alternately loved and hated it.
Sometimes the combination of idea, execution, and media place-
ment is so perfect that it is one of the most powerful weapons a
company can wield. I can't imagine a weary businessman who
had just driven four hours to a meeting passing that poster and
not thinking, "Screw it, next time I *will* take the plane."

As I wondered if I would ever return to the advertising agency
scene, we ground to a halt at the back of a long traffic jam.
Canberra doesn't usually have traffic jams but road construction
had temporarily brought the phenomenon to the capital city.
We crawled at a snail's pace into the city center. I gazed out the

window at the city and drove straight into the car in front of me. It was completely my fault—no two ways about it.

The driver of the car I had run into was already out of her vehicle and walking hurriedly toward me. I braced myself.

"Thank you, thank you, thank you," she said.

"Umm, what for?" I replied.

"Running into us. My kids have been driving me up the wall the whole way from Sydney. I'd told them if they continued to screw around then we'd have an accident. My son—the snotty brat—had just said, 'Yeah right, Mom,' when you hit us."

I looked into the backseat of her car and sure enough, there were two children sitting bolt upright, being very, very, well-behaved.

"It's a pleasure to be of service," I said.

Half an hour after our "accident," we pulled up outside the hotel I had booked over the Internet. Harry and Alex were beside themselves with excitement. I, on the other hand, was in a state of shock. The hotel had come recommended as "one of the premier establishments in Canberra." In reality, however, it was like a down-market motel that had been stuck in a 1970s time warp. It made me sad just standing in its foyer. By the elevators there was a glass case labeled "Some of our famous guests." Inside—and I swear I'm not making this up—were black-and-white photocopied pictures of four people. Not four hundred, or forty-four—but four. I can only assume they were famous in a different era as I'd never heard of any of them.

The room was appalling.

"Cool, this is great, Dad," said Harry, jumping up and down on the micro-sized double bed.

"Yeah. Awesome, Dad," added Alex. "Can I switch the TV on?"

I let them veg in front of the box while I ordered a cup of tea and some ice cream for the boys.

"I'll have a pot of tea please, with skim milk, and two bowls of ice cream. What flavors do you have?" I asked.

"Vanilla. We haven't got skim milk," I was told.

"What other flavors have you?"

"None."

"Okay, I'll have vanilla. Full cream milk is fine. How long will that be?"

"I'll be up in about forty-five minutes."

I refrained from asking how it could possibly take anyone forty-five minutes to make a pot of tea and put two scoops of ice cream into a couple of bowls. Instead I resolved to spend as little time as possible in the place.

I unpacked and got the guidebook out to plan our afternoon's activities. Once I'd got that sorted, I called Kate to let her know we had arrived, that everyone was fine, and that the boys had eaten lots of vegetables. Halfway through our conversation the doorbell rang so I handed the phone to the nearest boy—Harry—and went to open the door. The lads looked on wide-eyed in amazement as the man who clearly staffed both reception and room service brought in a tray with two bowls of ice cream on it. As I signed the receipt, Harry was filling his mom in on all the details in his best loud telephone voice: "Mom, our room is nice, the bed is humongous, there's a TV, and best of all, we've got a servant!"

The "servant" gave me a look that reminded me of the flight attendant on our recent flight to London.

"Harry, sweetheart, he's not a servant," I corrected.

"He's a slave?" Harry interrupted.

This time the "slave" shot me a look that reminded me of the type I'd got at Kindi Gym after Grace's helpful announcement. For a moment I was tempted to say, "No, darling, he's a humorless jerk with the style and elegance of a car crash." But I refrained, simply muttering, "He hasn't stayed in a hotel before. It's all very exciting for a five-year-old. Thanks for the tea."

As I escorted the slave to the door, I could hear Alex on the phone behind me. "Vegetables? No we haven't had any—or fruit. Dad's been fantastic. We had sweets in the car. Burgers for lunch. Then ice cream and candy. And we've just got some more ice cream delivered to the room. And Dad says we can have KFC for dinner."

After calming Kate down, we made our way into Canberra proper. Or tried to. Because Canberra is a new, purpose-built city, it was designed rather than evolving naturally. Unfortunately the town planners made the mistake of confusing "large, open, and green" with "good to live in." The city is well spaced out but precisely for that reason it lacks a center and therefore a heart.

Apparently Prince Philip once upset Canberrans when he remarked on an official visit to the city that Canberra had no soul. The travel writer Bill Bryson went one step further and suggested Canberra's official slogan should be "Canberra—why wait for death?" While I wouldn't go as far as either Bill or Phil, I could see where they were coming from. Canberra is—how can I put this?—rather open and suburban.

You would be wrong, however, to strike it off your list of places to visit. The city itself may be on the dull side of vibrant but the attractions within it are world-class—and numerous. I couldn't get the kids out of the interactive Science Museum or the Telstra Tower, which looks over the entire city and countryside beyond.

They even enjoyed the National Gallery. Not half as much as me, though. I couldn't believe the quality and sheer quantity of art they had on display. It was like someone had relocated the Musée d'Orsay to the outback. They even had Pollock's *Blue Poles* on display—one of my favorites of any painter.

We then did the National Portrait Gallery, where Alex was delighted to find a full-length portrait of Australian rugby star David Campese. I've said it before and I'll say it again—I love Australia. In an English portrait gallery you'd expect to wade through hundreds of pictures of guys on horses, looking like they were just off to subdue a few natives, or royalty with their noses in the air. In Oz you get a real mix: politicians, rugby players, businessmen, writers—an unaffected, interesting mix that truly reflects the country as a whole.

It's a matter of perspective, I suppose. I naturally see the good bits of Australia and actively look for the positive side of things. If, however, you come at it from an ex-colony/prison point of view, as many English people do, I can imagine there is enough wrong with it to keep you happy. My mother-in-law once memorably remarked, "I can't understand the point of Australia." Inadvertently or not, I think she hit the nail on the head. You either see the point, and it is the most remarkable place on earth, or you don't, and it is forever letting you down as it's never quite the same as New York or London. I'm sure none of this was going through Alex's and Harry's heads as they stuffed themselves on KFC while we toured Canberra stadium before we retired—as late as I could possibly arrange it—to the hotel.

I'd like to pretend that sleeping with your two young sons in a small double bed is fun, but it isn't. They had nine hours of deep, uninterrupted sleep while I lay awake all night. It reminded me of the time I slept in the garden shed of our house in London with Alex as "an adventure." He loved it. I, on the other hand, still have a small scar on my back from sleeping all night squashed against a hedge trimmer. After our slave—as I was now happy to think of him—brought us breakfast, we checked out and made for the Parliament buildings and war memorial. I was determined not to make the kids stay longer at any attraction than their natural attention span dictated. This may have meant we ended up doing whistle-stop tours of places where I would have loved to stay longer, but I like to think it also meant the kids enjoyed the trip rather than suffered it.

When we got back to Sydney that afternoon, I had the film from the disposable camera developed and gave a set of photos each to Alex and Harry as I tucked them up in bed that evening. Because of a lack of parental approval or affirmation when I was a young boy, I am forever overcompensating and telling my lads how wonderful they are and how proud of them I am. This night was very special to me. I'd just spent a heavenly couple of days with my sons and I felt enormously protective of them as I began my evening pep talk. "You're both such fantastic kids. Daddy is very—"

"Yeah, yeah, we know: very proud of us. Dad, you've said that so often it's lost all meaning," Alex interrupted.

The next day when I picked them up from school, one of Harry's classmates saw me across the playground crowded with parents and teachers. "Have you got a job yet, Mr. Marsh?" he yelled. "Harry says you have had to move your house because you have no money."

On top of Alex's comment the night before, I couldn't help remembering that a friend of mine recently told me that in trendy tree-hugging circles, embarrassing or crushing comments made to a child by an adult are described as "soul murder." I wondered if I could report my sons to the police for a reverse case of it.

With my self-esteem in shreds, I made my way to Harry's classroom. Before I could vent my annoyance, his teacher rushed up to me.

"Oh, Nigel, your boys did so enjoy the trip. Harry brought all his pictures and took the class through them at show and tell. Mr. Jansen tells me Alex did the same. They are lucky boys to spend so much time with their dad."

Glad someone thinks so.

Chapter 44

Folds Flat

THE PLAYGROUND MIGHT not have been the forum I would have chosen to discuss it, but Harry's friend had a point. We had had to move to a cheaper house. I don't want to pretend here—I'm well aware my situation was far more fortunate than most. But as much fun as I was having and as undoubtedly fortunate as we were, it didn't mean our finances were a laughing matter. We had a small lump sum that was eroding rapidly. The nanny, second car, and big house were only just affordable when I had a job; without one they all had to go.

I didn't mind moving to a cheaper place, but it wasn't actually that easy to find somewhere that was close enough for the kids not to have to move schools and big enough—and within our new price range. Having four kids does tend to limit your options.

We eventually found a place and to my mind it was perfect. Kate suspects I would have said this about any house in Sydney because I am so biased. Given it was near the school and beaches, I just couldn't see any justifiable reason to complain. But it was much smaller, so we had to get rid of a lot of stuff. I actually found this incredibly enjoyable. I hate clutter and it was a wonderful excuse to do what I'd wanted to do anyway.

It's amazing how much crap you end up carting around as a family unless you are rigorous about it. We currently pay hundreds of dollars a year to keep two crates in a storage facility in London. For the life of us, Kate and I can no longer remember what is in them, although at the time it must have seemed important for us to pay to keep it. I was determined not to make the same mistake this time. "If in doubt, chuck it out" had been our motto for the move. The local Goodwill didn't know whether it was Christmas or Easter.

A side benefit of the move was that it gave me a chance to indulge a private fantasy I'd been nursing ever since I read about a movement that had sprung up in San Francisco a few years earlier. To cut a long story short, this group dedicates itself to committing frequent and regular random acts of "kindness." They started with the simple act of paying for the cars behind them at the bridge tollbooths. It struck me as a wonderful way of increasing world happiness and I'd long since secretly wanted to try it.

My chance came the day before the move. I was taking Grace and Eve for one last run in the double baby jogger. They were now three and getting too big for it, and there was nowhere to store it in the new house. As I approached Clovelly beach, I ran past a young woman struggling to get a stroller out of the back of her car. Inside the car were two babies. I stopped running and inquired in a voice as far as possible removed from that of a stalker, "Excuse me, are they twins?"

"Yes," she said.

"Gorgeous. How old?"

"Eleven months," she replied.

"Hope you don't mind me asking, but would you by any chance want a double jogger?" I felt more than a little stupid at this point.

"What do you mean?"

"A double jogger. This double jogger."

"Er . . . I'd love it. I used to run before these two were born but I haven't been able to find the time to do it since. This stroller is bloody useless as well. I can hardly get it out of the car, let alone run and push it. I've always wondered if those jogger things were as good as they looked. Can you take it on the beach?"

"Yep."

"And you can actually *run* behind it?"

"Yep—I've done races with it."

"Does it fold flat?"

"In about fifteen seconds, once you've got the hang of it."

"How much would you want for it? Don't they cost six hundred bucks? I haven't got that sort of money."

"Nothing."

"Nothing?"

"Nothing."

"Are you sure?"

"Sure."

"When could I pick it up?"

"I'll help you get your girls in it now if you like."

"Really?"

"Really."

I got Grace and Eve out of the jogger and showed her how to strap her girls into the seats.

The whole conversation took less than five minutes. As I walked my twins up the hill toward home, I realized I hadn't even got the lady's name or number. As random acts go, it was pretty random. I suppose I was lucky, as I could have got a smack in the mouth or a hearty "Shove off, you patronizing bastard." But I didn't, and without wanting to sound like I've got a messiah complex, it felt bloody wonderful.

Chapter 45

Lenny Bruce

WITH OUR HOUSE MOVE over and no further trips planned, we settled into a routine of enjoyable domesticity. The world of work seemed several light-years away. Kate and I started not just going out again but planning to go out. There is a big difference. Previously a suggestion of an evening out was almost always met by me with a "Going out with whom? Tonight? Jesus, when were you going to tell me? I can't stay out late, I've got a meeting in the morning." Blah blah blah, you know the sort of thing. Not so much "soul murder" as "relationship murder."

These days we spent time actually planning a social life in advance. It's remarkable how much free entertainment is available in Sydney if you look for it. It is equally surprising how far a limited budget can stretch if you're smart about it. We were seeing so many concerts and plays on our tight budget that I was half considering applying for a job as a paupers' art critic with the *Herald*.

Importantly, this newfound lust for a varied and stimulating social life enabled me to get back in touch with another lapsed passion—stand-up comedy. My love affair with comedy predates even my love affair with running. In London I used to see stand-up at least twice a week, yet I hadn't been once since arriving in Australia. We arranged to go to a show one weekend.

The evening had a strange effect on me. I'm a harsh judge of comedians, and two of the three acts on offer were distinctly ho-hum—lots of swearing and jokes about student days, screwing, and pot smoking. Embarrassing, frankly.

Just as I was beginning to think I had outgrown stand-up comedy or that Australia just had lousy acts, the last comedian came on. From his first words—a freewheeling rant about how boy bands should be called boy choirs as they don't play instruments—it was clear he was on fire. He slayed the audience. For twenty minutes straight everyone in the pub was roaring and yelling. He just took the laughs, rode them, and flung back yet more ammo to keep the hilarity boiling. He was in total control of a room full of people who five minutes ago had never heard of him. It was quite a performance, yet all I could think was how much I pitied his girlfriend.

My own stint as a stand-up comic started shortly after my career as a squash coach ended. When I was doing stand-up, I was impossible to live with. I was lucky enough to be doing well at it, but this luck didn't extend to Kate. For some bizarre reason, I banned her from attending any of my gigs.

Instead of the performance itself she got the after-show: a thoroughly unfair trade. I'm not sure it's possible to properly describe to someone who hasn't done it what it's like for a comic to successfully capture his audience. It's like sex, winning the lottery, and scoring the winning goal in the World Cup final all rolled into one. It gets even better if you wrote all your own material and you suffer from unresolved childhood issues that give you an unhealthy need for public shows of affection and praise.

On one particular night, I was having such a fantastic show that I actually ended my set, "My name is Nigel Marsh, watch out for my show on Channel Four this October. Thank you for being such a good audience, good night." They cheered all the more thinking that they were witnessing an up-and-coming TV star. The thing is, it was complete bullshit. I made it up. An out-and-out lie. There was no TV series. There was more chance of me playing for England than me ever appearing on TV. But at the time it was real. I believed it. I was Lenny Bruce. I was so in character at that particular moment that if I'd been offered a TV series of my own I wouldn't even have been surprised.

And that is where the problems started—for Kate, anyway. I would get home to our apartment and be mildly surprised to find that the world's media wasn't camped on my doorstep and downright outraged that Kate hadn't put up banners and hired a brass band for the return of the conquering hero. The coming down from my Lenny Bruce moment was not a good spectator sport and unfortunately for Kate she was the only one in that particular audience. Add in some Olympic-standard drinking and it all gets pretty ugly.

My mood was made worse by the fact that I knew I was living a lie. You see, I didn't just lie at the end of my act—I lied to get the gigs as well. I hadn't set out to lie, but the first time I called up to arrange a spot hadn't been a success.

"Hi, I'd like to do a gig at your stand-up night," I said on the phone to the owner of a famous North London pub.

"OK, mate, three weeks Wednesday we've got one slot left. How many gigs have you done?" he replied.

"Uh . . . none. This will be my first time."

"First time? You never done this before?"

"Uh . . . no."

"Don't know about your act, mate, but you certainly sound like a bloody comedian to me," he said before hanging up.

Clearly a bit of bluffing was needed. Reminding myself of my squash coaching experience, I looked through the paper for another pub that had comedy nights. I called one at random—an inner-city bar just off Oxford Street.

"Hi, I'm calling to book a spot at one of your comedy nights."

"Good timing, I've just had a guy cancel on me. Are you free next Thursday?"

"Yes."

"Right. Wait, you're not one of those first-time amateurs, are you? We don't do those anymore since the last one ran off the stage when the audience started throwing bottles at him. Poor jerk got hit by a couple and started crying on stage. Pathetic."

"Sounds tragic, all right," I said, thinking of both myself and the poor jerk.

"How many have you done?" he asked,

I felt my Lenny Bruce complex take over. "Don't know. Stopped counting at a hundred. Probably two hundred or so by now," I lied.

"Excellent, in that case I'll bump you up the bill a bit. Are you all right going on second?"

"Yes," I lied again.

"Can you give me fifteen minutes?"

"I'll have to cut some good stuff out, but sure, if that's the time you want," I lied yet again. Listen to me, I'm a bloody schizophrenic. I haven't got five minutes of material, let alone fifteen. Next thing I know I'll be telling him I'm Lenny Bruce.

"What did you say your name was?" he asked.

"Lenny Bruce," I replied.

"Very funny. Your real one."

"Oh, Nigel Marsh," I confessed.

Bizarrely, on the night itself I avoided any bottle throwing. In fact I even got a couple of big laughs and a half-decent round of applause at the end. From then on whenever I called to book a spot, I would lie about my experience. It meant I rarely got turned down but it played havoc with my nerves. I wasn't just petrified about dying on stage, I was petrified that the lies I told in each booking conversation would be revealed in some hideously humiliating way. But I never did die on stage or get found out. Every week I thought that would be it, but it never was. The pressure built to unbearable proportions so I decided to quit while I was ahead. "Bottled it" was how Kate supportively phrased it.

Cowardice or not, the weird thing was I enjoyed *telling* people I used to do stand-up more than I enjoyed *doing* stand-up. It was a damn sight easier as well. Remembering these stories brought me to my senses. After a brief moment of reflection I realized there is no sense trying to relive absolutely everything good about your past—some things belong there. Comedy performing, like drinking, is probably one of them. I decided to stick to running instead.

Chapter 46
One-legged Faker

I CAN PINPOINT THE precise moment when I realized my transformation from "Executive Dad" to "Guy Who Doesn't Work" was complete. It happened one morning when I was in our bathroom. I couldn't find any toothpaste.

"Kate, where's the toothpaste?" I yelled.

"We've run out. Could you please buy some for us today?"

"We can't have run out. I've got about a hundred of those small ones from British Airlines and Qantas somewhere."

"'Fraid not, I finished the last one yesterday."

Shit, I thought, I'm actually going to have to buy some toothpaste. Since my previous job involved a lot of travel, I hadn't paid for any toothpaste—or shampoo, come to think of it—for over a year. Hotels and airlines were so wonderfully generous with stuff like that—especially when you were traveling in business class. It may seem like a trivial event, but to me it triggered a whole series of thoughts.

Except for the weddings, I hadn't worn a tie or jacket in the last nine months. Eve had drawn all over my just-completed sketchbook the week before and I hadn't lost my temper. Harry had taken to creeping out of his bunk bed in the middle of the night and sleeping under our bed. Rather than shouting at him, the third time it happened I lay down on the floor next to him and asked him why he did it. "Because I don't like rectangles, Daddy," was his reply. At least he was still using his real name. Grace was warming to me and on the weekend had even hugged me and said, "Daddy, I'm not a vile children, really." I—and the family—really, genuinely had changed.

I'm not suggesting I was even remotely approaching the foothills of being perfect. The kids' nickname for me was still "Shirker Tensing." The house would ring out with the cries of "Shirker! Shirker! Mom wants you!" whenever I was dodging my parental chores. My most regular shirk was to offer to "put the bath on" whenever dinnertime got just a little too awful. Then I would slip off to the bathroom, turn the taps on, and then watch the bath fill as if this act was helping in some way. It drove Kate up the wall. I knew when I was in real trouble because she used my name at the end of a rant. "Bloody hell, what have you been doing all this time?" is a million miles of anger away from "Bloody hell, what have you been doing all this time, *Nigel*?"

It wasn't just my shirking that caused tension. My goal-focused nature had its downsides as well. This was no more apparent than when the time came for Kate, Alex, and I to do the Bridge Run. It was the first race we were doing together and I was enormously excited. Unfortunately, it is likely to remain the only race we have done together.

The race itself was heavenly. I love Alex beyond words and warming up with him on the North Sydney Oval before the starter's gun is still one of my all-time favorite memories. It was precisely the type of occasion that makes me adore Sydney— thousands of happy people sharing an experience together in the most wonderful setting in the most gorgeous weather. I found running on the actual blue line of the 2000 Olympics an amazing, fantasy-inducing event. Half the time I wasn't Nigel Marsh, or even Lenny Bruce, but a cross between Maurice Greene and Carl Lewis. And therein lay the problem. While the race itself may have been fabulous, the ending was suboptimal.

To my utter shame, I feel my happiness, enthusiasm, and private fantasies may have led me to "encourage" my running partners just a little bit too much. As we crossed the finishing line together at the steps of the Opera House, Alex's legs started to buckle and his face turned deathly white. A race marshal rushed to his aid.

"This boy has been pushed far too hard, he's badly dehydrated. We need to get him to the medical tent. Where's his father?" he said.

"I think he's over there," I said, pointing in as vague a way as possible. "He said he would be gone for a while. I'll look after the kid until he returns. Bloody irresponsible if you ask me."

Kate, God bless her, didn't blow my cover and a cup of water and a handful of jelly beans later, Alex was released from the medical tent in good health and high spirits at having completed the course. I, on the other hand, rightly got the tongue-lashing of my life, hence my suspicion that it may be a while until we do a family event like that again.

I wouldn't want you to think Kate was perfect herself, though. For the twelve years I have lived with her, she has always taken the tea bag out of her cup and, rather than put it in the garbage, she has placed it on the kitchen countertop next to the garbage. It is beyond my quite considerable powers of comprehension to understand what could possibly make someone do something so moronic, so often, for so long. Especially after the fights we have had about it. Then again, it is entirely possible that with some sort of twisted logic she does it *because* it irritates the shit out of me. As I've said before, women can be so cruel.

These imperfections apart, however, the Marsh family had found a very nice balance indeed, thank you very much. I was swimming, surfing, running, sketching, and writing as much as I wanted, while at the same time being an involved and improving husband and father. I was keeping the weight off and, most important of all, I was still off the booze. This was an enormously significant change—and in all probability the factor that had enabled and continued to enable the other changes to take place in my life.

Giving up drinking is a difficult subject to talk about, let alone write about. People's reactions are so completely polarizing. One group is enormously supportive—thank you to all those concerned, especially Kate—while another group is actively destructive.

This latter group devotes considerable energy to trying every conceivable way to make you drink. "Go on, just have one. How can one hurt?" they say. This may seem slightly fantastic, but it is true. What makes it all the stranger is that among their numbers are people who are supposedly close to you and care for you the most. I'm not blaming these people. It is a complex issue. Part of it, I'm sure, stems from the discomfort of having someone so close change so fundamentally. It can be a bit unnerving if all you've ever done together is get drunk in pubs to then have to find something else to do or face the awkward reality that the friendship was only drink-deep, so to speak.

There is, however, a group who are far worse. These are the people who are seemingly tormented with a compulsion to prove that you didn't have a drinking problem in the first place. Initially it took a while for me to spot them, but as the months went by I was able see them coming a mile off. They'd usually start off slow and then build into it.

"I hear you stopped drinking, Nige," they'd say to me.

"Uh, yeah," I'd reply.

"Why'd you do it?"

"Just had enough of it, mate."

"Really? I thought you loved a drop."

"Truth is, I did, but I've got a bit of an issue with it, so I've decided my drinking days are over."

"Bit of an issue? What do you mean?"

"Well, I don't want to go on about it, but I just started to find it was becoming too important in my life so I decided to stop before it got totally out of hand."

"You're not saying you're an alcoholic, are you?"

"Actually, now you mention it, yes. But I . . ."

"You're not an alcoholic. My brother, now he was a real alcoholic. Ran someone over when he was drunk on his way back home from work one day, spent a year in jail. Bottle of whisky before lunch for twenty years before he finally kicked it."

"Uh, well, I'm glad he's sober now."

"Yeah, and my pal Simon—he had a real problem. He'd wet himself at night, sleep with prostitutes, get into fights, go on benders that lasted for five days!" This last bit would be emphasized with the type of pride and pleasure normally associated with telling someone you'd just become a father or won gold at the Olympics.

"How awful. Is he all right now?"

"Dunno, haven't seen him in a while, but take my other friend, Jane. She's a scream, real whack-o. Her husband doesn't know it, but she's added a 'pick-me-up' to her morning tea for years. Last Christmas he noticed her hands shaking and she had to go through this whole charade of pretending to go to the doctor and then making up some story about a potentially life-threatening hereditary shaking disease. Silly bastard believes her and he's devastated. Now *that's* a real drinking problem! I've never even seen you be sick. You don't even drink before lunch. You're a lightweight, pal. Take the guy I worked with last year . . ." And so it would go on.

The stories differed, but the intent didn't. I was somehow offending these people's sense of what a "real" drunk's story should be. I wasn't a professional drunk—I was merely third division. Pathetic. My life hadn't gone off the rails enough for them. If only I could have an affair, lose my job, or maim someone in a car accident, I'd be a first-class guy. It just didn't impress these people that I stopped before a dramatic disaster befell me. It was weird. Like touring a hospital ward and haranguing amputees with stories about people who'd lost two legs. Two! Not one like you, you one-legged faker.

The vocal insistence of this group is almost worse than their breathtaking disregard for your well-being. I'm relaxed about my failure to qualify in their eyes as a real drunk. Delighted, in fact. I couldn't be happier that the story of my addiction is boringly tame. On one level I'm pleased to tell it—if it helps one person recognize he had a problem earlier than he would have if he believed he had to be a tramp on the streets before he qualified, then I'll actually have done some good. The point is, I don't really like talking about it. But these people are like a dog with a bone and feel the need to publicly go on and on and on about it.

Of course in the end the problem isn't how other people react; it is the internal battle that is the key. I was finding it easier and easier as the months passed, but it was still a subject I thought about most days. Unlike many alcoholics, I find the "never again" notion helpful, not off-putting. The classic syndrome is taking "one day at a time" because the thought of not drinking ever again is deemed just too overwhelming an idea to cope with. Whatever works for the individual, I say.

Without wanting to tempt fate by making any grand pronouncements, I'm increasingly comfortable in potentially difficult drinking situations and am enjoying the sober life in general. That isn't to say that there aren't regular challenges. Only a few weeks ago, as I was walking across the parking lot of a local school to the AA meeting held in its basement, I bumped into an old business colleague. He wasn't fat, hadn't yet reached forty, and, far from being fired, ran the largest and most success-ful advertising agency in Sydney.

"Hi, Jim," I said. "What are you doing here?"

"Oh, I'm here every Saturday morning. This is where Olivia comes for her ballet classes. They're held in the hall on the first floor. What are you doing here, Nigel? Are Grace and Eve taking up ballet?"

"Uh, no . . . I'm going to the AA meeting in the basement."

Embarrassing moments like this aside, I was actually loving my new life. It may have taken nine months, but all in all I had eventually found (or created) a set of circumstances I was totally happy with and had no desire to change.

Almost immediately upon coming to this realization, disaster struck.

In September I was offered a job.

Chapter 47

Anaïs Nin

AT LEAST I COULDN'T complain about not having enough time to think through the job offer. For the next week, every swim, run, or dinnertime was spent laboriously analyzing the pros and cons of a return to the treadmill. The job being offered was fantastic and in my former life I would have leapt at. It involved running a well-known and successful communications company. Of that type of job it didn't really get better. What's more, I had friends in the company. One of my partners would be Todd, an ex-colleague from my previous role whom I admired both professionally and personally. He had a certain something about him that suggested he hadn't yet given up and become a total corporate squirrel. A couple of years before, he'd taken three months off work and climbed to the summit of Mount Everest. Solo.

I also loved how he took his personal values to work. On one memorable occasion a client of ours had been attempting to excuse her appalling behavior by saying that she wasn't like that at home, only at work. Todd replied, "Susan, if you are an asshole *at work* it doesn't mean you are an asshole at work—it means you are an asshole."

It would be good to hook up with him again. Beyond old friends, however, was the fact that the job was a real leadership role. It offered me a chance to make a difference. I've always remembered a story I read in a biography of the British prime minister William Gladstone. He kept a diary recording how he used each fifteen minutes of his life so when he was called to account at the Pearly Gates he would have the evidence that he hadn't wasted the divine gift of a life. I'm not quite as rigorous as Gladstone, but I do want to look back and feel I've used my four score and ten well—if I get that long.

Also, as much as I was loving time off work and my newfound "man around the playground" persona, the money was running out and the kids were still a bit young to become panhandlers. I was coming around to the idea of going back to work. I had made some dramatic improvements in my life—but hadn't yet faced the biggest issue.

Work-life balance.

I had found that, unlike many men, I could enjoy not working. But on the balance front all I'd really found out was that I was good at juggling life and work when I didn't have any work to juggle. But I knew I had to go back to work soon. The bigger question, therefore, was could I go back to work and retain the life changes and the attitude I had come to value deeply over the last few months? That seemed to be the biggest challenge of all.

If I were to limit myself to the easier challenges (swimming, losing a bit of weight), my time off might turn out to have been a period when I made a few minor adjustments that did a bit of good but that ultimately had no dramatic bearing on my and my family's longer-term welfare—fundamentally an excellent, very long vacation, rather than the permanently life-changing event I wanted it to be. But I'd tackled some harder issues this year, too, and surely if I could crack the booze issue, I could crack the balance one. I was, after all, good at resolutions. My time off had shown me that if I really set my mind to something I could usually do it. Whatever it was.

Deep down I wanted the job. But I decided that I would take it only if I made a resolution to control the impact it would have on my broader life. This would be no small step. For me a resolution should not be an exercise in wishful thinking. To my mind, if I'm not prepared to devote a year's worth of dedicated and persistent time and energy to a particular goal then I haven't actually made a resolution.

Yet I couldn't get rid of the nagging doubts. What about the effect it might really have on the family? I didn't want to revert to being the dad in a suit who grumpily dropped his kids off at school in the morning without so much as a preoccupied glance backward. Would Grace start calling me "poo-poo head" again? Would Harry's pictures start coming back from school with different names on them? Would I stay off the booze? Get fat? Would I manage to complete the Bondi to Bronte ocean race? What about the lifeguard course and exam I'd signed up to take in October? Or the Rugby World Cup games I'd arranged to go to with Alex? We had plane tickets and hotel reservations to follow the England team around the country on an extended

Lad and Dad trip in November. Would we still go to the games? Would this mean I would have no time to write? Or draw? Or surf?

Irrespective of how good the new firm was, did I really want to get back into an industry that so often polluted the ether with a steady steam of mindless shit? Just that morning I'd caught an ad on TV that made me groan and hold my head. "Have we gone mad? It's carpet madness at Carpet Universe! You'd be insane not to check out our crazy, crazy prices. Yes, we've gone mental. You'd be nutty if you didn't take advantage of our loony deals!" All delivered by an idiot shouting at the top of his lungs.

The week before I'd seen two other ads, both of which I couldn't for the life of me figure out—not just what they were about, but what they were selling or who they were for. For the last few months I had been reading the paper from cover to cover every day, yet on most days I hadn't read, or even noticed, one single ad.

Companies and their advertising agencies seem to have an almost paranoid fear of being honest about their products and the real role they play in people's lives. On the rare occasions when a company does speak honestly and with a bit of charm and empathy, it leaps out at you. And here's the rub—the more I hated the business, the more I wanted to get back into it. We could do it better. I wanted to do it better. Not just the end product bit—the ads—but also the bit that produced the end product bit. People.

At the start of my previous job I'd given an interview to the press where I was asked what I thought the primary role of a CEO was. I replied that I viewed my primary role as "providing meaning." They then did a piece about the whacky theologian CEO. Trouble was, I meant it then and I mean it now.

I believe a CEO's role is to provide meaningful employment. That doesn't mean he or she doesn't have to make the numbers or make difficult decisions. It means he or she has to provide a point for the employees. And for me this point has to be something more involving than "I'd like you all to work very hard at a job you don't like much to make some shareholders you'll never meet richer." (I'd understand if you don't believe me, but I have been in that very presentation. I think the man who delivered the speech was actually disappointed when, at the end of his piece, the audience—all of whom, including me, weren't shareholders—didn't stand up and cheer.) I had loved my previous CEO role and was excited about another one. I believed I had something to offer in this field and found it difficult to imagine passing up this chance to potentially make a difference.

Anaïs Nin once remarked that life expands or contracts in direct proportion to one's courage. If I had learned only one thing from my time off, it was that I vehemently agree with her sentiment. I didn't want to settle for a life of regret and disappointment. I passionately believe that if you eradicate your limiting assumptions, raise your expectations, and work damn hard at your goals, it's remarkable what you can achieve. If you have the right attitude you can have a damn good laugh while you're at it as well. I wanted to expand my footprint on the world, not shrink it. You are, after all, dead a long time. The more I thought about it, the closer I came to taking the leap and getting back on the treadmill to see if I could actually crack the work-life dilemma and be a success both in my job and at home.

However, in the middle of these self-indulgent deliberations, real disaster struck.

Chapter 48

Granfie

MOM CALLED ME from England to inform me that my dad had fallen desperately ill. He had been diagnosed with Parkinson's disease over ten years earlier and until now, a strictly monitored drug regime had kept the condition to a frustrating but manageable state. Apparently things had dramatically declined overnight to such an extent that he'd had to be moved to a hospital. Understandably, Mom sounded dreadfully upset.

I made the snap decision that I would go and see them immediately. Mom was overwhelmed when I told her. The moment I put the phone down I made another decision—I would take Alex with me. Granfie, as my kids called him, had always adored Alex and lavished him with the type of attention and praise I rarely, if ever, received. We were living proof of the cliché that a grandparent is able to express love more easily to a grandchild than to his own child.

Mom and Dad had invited Alex to Somerset for a number of weekends by himself. On each occasion he was treated like a king, taken fishing, played endless games, fed treats—basically spoiled rotten. He returned after each trip with a book done by his granny, detailing each day's activities including photos stuck to the pages at all the critical moments. A real bond existed between them, and I couldn't bear the thought of Alex not seeing his granddad again. Besides, part of me thought that seeing Alex might actually help my dad.

Deciding to go was one thing. Arranging the trip was another thing entirely. The only flight that left the next day went via Singapore *and* Rome, with a combined travel time of a little over thirty hours. Once that was booked, I had Alex's headmistress to negotiate. To be fair, she was a champ. Our flights had Alex returning the day before the school play and so we struck a deal: I could take him out of school for the week as long as I guaranteed I would make him practice his lines every day.

After some hasty packing we jumped in a taxi and barely hours after the initial phone conversation we were checking in for the first leg of the marathon journey to Somerset, England. We may have been flying economy, but I still had a shiny airline frequent-flyer card that was yet to be downgraded. To the computer, I was still superexec, not superdad. Having said that, I think the system registered that my circumstances had changed slightly after I spent two hours in the first-class lounge wearing shorts and a T-shirt and playing Battleship with Alex.

The journey was uncomfortable and long and made longer still by delays at every stopover. The time spent with Alex, though, was simply magical. I was so proud of him. He was a wonderful companion. It didn't matter to me if we were stuck in the Rome airport for a week, it was just so much fun being with my elder son. The irony wasn't lost on me. We, father and son, were traveling arm in arm to see my own father whom I had never been close to. We were going to spend the type of week together, one-on-one, that I had never had with my father as an adult, let alone as a child.

Money was getting tight, so at Heathrow we reverted to "Tasmanian Rules" and rented the cheapest vehicle in the entire airport. It is actually quite difficult to rent the cheapest car. Whether it is because they work on commission or because they simply can't believe you don't want comfort, the Eurocar and Budget salespeople of the world challenge themselves to rent you their best vehicle. To Ford's credit, the Focus we ended up with may have had the power and comfort of a lawn mower, but it didn't break down once, and boy was it cheap.

When we arrived in Somerset, it was midnight. Mom was delighted to see us and smothered Alex in hugs. It was too late to visit the hospital, so we put Alex to bed and Mom and I shared a pot of tea while she filled in the details. Dad was in Frenchay Hospital in Bristol, about forty miles away. He was extremely confused and had lost all mobility. He was also having enormous difficulty talking beyond the simplest remarks. The specialist was attempting to find a new drug regime that would arrest the decline and bring some improvement. It was acknowledged that recovery would not be complete, if there was any improvement at all.

But none of the descriptions adequately prepared me for the reality. Seeing my dad the next day was simply heartrending. With respect to England's National Health Service, the ward was like a Crimean War hospital tent. No privacy, no comforts, just two rows of iron beds with sick people in them. Alex was a lifesaver.

"Is it good in here, Granfie?" he asked cheerfully.

No answer.

"When are you going to get your knowledge back, Granfie?" he went on.

No answer.

"I'll chat to the doctor and get you a TV, Granfie. There's a *Simpsons* special on this weekend."

No answer.

And so on. For half an hour. Apart from taking Dad to the bathroom twice, I was a bit player in the visit.

Walking to the car later, Alex took my hand. "Don't be sad, Daddy, Granfie's getting old."

Beyond the sadness, it just felt so unfair. Dad had had an extremely humble upbringing. His early life was far from easy and frequently marked with tragedy. His own father died young after a long illness. Both his sisters also died young in tragic circumstances, and Dad was left an only child with a mom who never recovered from the hand that life had dealt her. Dad had to spend every hour he wasn't at school or sleeping working in the pub where Nanna was a barmaid. When the draft came, it was a step up for Dad, as opposed to almost all his contemporaries, for whom it was a drop in their living standards. Dad was a man with a strong sense of duty; he stayed in the Royal Navy for thirty-two years. Then he took a role in the United Nations. Just seven more years until he could allow himself to relax and enjoy a well-earned retirement with his wife. Then, bang—this.

Kate had always clicked with Dad, saying he had such a glint in his eye and an ever-present, dry, gentle humor. He may have been light on the huggy-kissy stuff to his sons, but he was a good man who had strived all his life to do the right thing, irrespective of how hard he had personally found it.

Latter-day notions of chasing personal happiness would have made Dad laugh. You had to do your duty. If that made you happy, fine. If that made you miserable, fine. While this could lend him a hard edge, I had an enormous amount to thank him for. At every step of the way he was there doing his best for me. He may not have been telling me, but he was doing it, making the sacrifices, paying his dues, spurning easy popularity, and religiously sticking to his guns. He brought my brother and me up well. I loved him. I was miserable. It was only day one of the visit and I was a basket case. *Snap out of it, Nigel,* I thought.

Chapter 49

Mrs. Sargeant

THE WEEK WAS emotionally rewarding, though, as well as draining. Apart from time with Alex, I was also having the quality time with Mom that I'd never had. Nine months before, I'd thought I could create this type of experience by taking her out to a fancy dinner. I realized now that most of the time, important moments happen when they will, not when you decide you want them to.

I cringe at all the times in the past I must have forced matters in the hope of an emotionally rewarding exchange. Then again, if you hardly spend any time with someone you haven't got much choice but to treasure those rare moments when you're together. Or, as the American self-help gurus say, "You need quantity time for quality time." On the second day, I drove Alex over to stay with his cousins, so it was just Mom and I in the house. Time with her was as happy as visits to Dad were sad. Most days I drove Mom with me to Bristol. We'd spend the journeys reminiscing, retelling favorite family stories even though we'd told them hundreds of times before.

Mom surprised me on one trip with a story she had never told before. The story wasn't the surprise—indeed, I starred in it—it was the fact that she was telling it. You see, we'd never mentioned it once in the thirty or so years since it happened.

The setting was the terraced house in Yeovil where we lived when I was a kid. My bedroom was at the back of the house and looked over the yard between our row of houses and the row behind us. In fact, my bedroom window looked directly into the bedroom window of the couple who lived at number 17, the Sargeants. I'd been given a pair of binoculars for Christmas and, in my defense, I didn't have many things to look at. It seemed natural to rest my elbows on the windowsill and look through them at Mrs. Sargeant as she got dressed in the mornings.

One such morning, she looked my way and paused. She peered intently in my direction. She moved closer to her window to get a better look. She was obviously going to spot me if I didn't move soon. Problem was, I'd been brought up in a military family and one of my childhood lessons learned at Dad's knee was that when a flare went up in the jungle you never dived for cover, as the movement would give you away. It was the people who stayed completely still even when they were momentarily bathed in light who weren't spotted. They were simply mistaken for a bush or a tree.

With this theory as my guide, I stayed still. Mrs. Sargeant was now right at her window and she was looking directly at me with an outraged expression on her face. I stayed as still as a statue, hoping to be mistaken for something other than a perverted adolescent. Mrs. Sargeant called over her shoulder to her husband, who came running into the room. Mrs. Sargeant pointed at me. Mr. Sargeant recoiled in horror as he saw his neighbor's ten-year-old son staring at his naked wife through a pair of binoculars. He made a rather rude sign and mouthed something even ruder. I clung to my military theory and didn't move a muscle. Mr. Sargeant left the room. I heard the phone ring and Mom pick it up. I could hear one side of the conversation.

"How dare you, Mr. Sargeant. My son would never do such a thing. If your wife has ugly fantasies about my boy, that's her problem, not Nigel's. I know for a fact he's upstairs doing his homework. If I were you I'd spend more time getting Brenda to stop parading naked by her window than slandering your neighbors."

And I still didn't move. I didn't move when Mom came into my room. Or even when she stood next to me looking out the window at both Mr. and Mrs. Sargeant pointing back at me as I remained frozen, with my elbows resting on the sill and my eyes glued to the binoculars. So much for the bloody military. Perhaps it's not surprising, but I'm the only Marsh for a couple of generations who hasn't signed up.

As Mom told this story, I was surprised by my reaction. I found myself laughing. Really laughing, as if I were hearing a friend tell a funny story, not cringing while a parent revealed a shameful secret. The fact that we both knew the story in question didn't matter. It was wonderful: The harder I laughed, the harder Mom did. By the time she had finished with Mrs. Sargeant, we were both giggling like teenagers. To this day I feel that that moment was a permanent breakthrough in our relationship. Strange how unexpected benefits come from the least likely events—it's almost enough to give lechery a good name.

On the last day of our U.K. stay, I wanted to visit Dad alone, without having to worry about either Alex or Mom. Although the doctors told me his condition wasn't life-threatening, I had an awful feeling that this was going to be our last good-bye. After my usual forced cheery comments dried up, this time I didn't fall silent. Instead, I started mumbling about how much I loved him, admired him, had always looked up to him, wanted him to get better, and would be thinking of him every day in Australia.

To my surprise, Dad stopped me. He raised his arm and placed a shaking hand on my wrist. He was looking me directly in the eye. He found it difficult to speak and his words were slow and faint. I leaned forward to listen.

"Means so much to me that you came, Nigel . . . and that you brought that fine boy. . . . I'm so very proud of you. . . . I always have been. . . . Your mother and I adore Kate and the kids. . . . It makes us so happy to hear of your progress in Australia."

It was like a different man was talking. Dad never spoke like this. When I had told him I was getting married to Kate, he berated me for not having a good enough job. When I'd told him we were having twins, he'd asked me how on earth I thought I could afford so many kids. When I was promoted to my last job, he asked me if it would be in the *Times*. Having to admit it wouldn't even be in *Campaign* magazine nicely made sure I didn't get too cocky.

I didn't know how to react. Or rather I did. I cried. Not just then, but walking to the car. And in the parking lot. On the drive home, I had to pull over because I couldn't stop crying. Just when I managed to stop, I started all over again when I got home and Mom asked me how it went. I'm loath to admit it, but I'm crying writing this now. You look pretty stupid at the traffic lights in a Ford Focus blubbering like a baby or writing in

256

a Bronte beach café with tears pouring down your face. Perhaps emotional repression isn't such a bad thing after all.

On the journey home to Australia I reflected again on the choice facing me. Whether it was this job or another, I would have to start earning again soon. If I were to go back to running an advertising agency I could think of few better jobs than this one. They prided themselves on their integrity and thoughtfulness and besides, the founder—Leo Burnett—seemed a man after my own heart, one of his more famous quotes being, "Advertising is somewhat less than the main purpose of human existence." Precisely.

After six hours thrashing around in yet another hideously uncomfortable BA seat, I struck a deal with myself. I blame all those self-help books I've read. The deal was that I would write down on paper a detailed description of the type of person and boss I wanted to be, and the type of family and company I would be proud to be a part of. I would then use this tangible commitment as a way to help me ensure that the positive changes I had undergone over the last nine months were permanent, not just forgotten as soon as I returned to the office.

Before I dealt with setting foot back in an office, I had to cope with the reactions of those around me to my decision to go back. For a woman who'd recently been forced to get rid of the nanny, pack up the family, and move to a smaller place, Kate was remarkably understanding about being left to deal with it all on her own. While she didn't complain about her lot—my mother rather charmingly suggested she probably couldn't wait to get me out of the house—she did express serious concern that my life changes would prove temporary once I got back to work.

However, Kate's worries about my return to the workplace were easy to deal with in comparison to the reactions of others.

They divided into a number of camps, the two worst being the Patronizers and the Jealousites. The first group's reaction was characterized by a "I see the boy has finally come to his senses—I told you it was just a short-term affectation" type of sentiment, while the latter group's was more along the lines of "You've had a year off that we never had so we secretly hope you have a really bad time now to make up for the months of freedom that we resent you for."

Among such mean-spirited and gossipy reactions the response of my swimming chums was wonderfully refreshing. "Just because you've wimped out of your sea change experiment doesn't mean you've got an excuse to wimp out of the sea," was how one of them supportively put it as she expressed their common fear that I would stop my swimming training and, worst of all, not complete the ocean race.

Having absorbed the gamut of reactions, I wrote my "personal contract" the day before I was to return to the office. Then I showed it to Kate. No one else has seen it. No one else will. We were both rather pleased with it.

Writing it was one thing—living it was a different matter entirely.

Chapter 50

House of Pain

IT WOULD BE FAIR to say my return to the treadmill wasn't exactly smooth. I prepared for my first day with excitement. We hadn't had time to replace the car we'd sold and as I was still working out how to get from Clovelly to McMahons Point, on the north shore of Sydney Harbor, by public transport in less than two hours, I had called a taxi. The idea was that a relaxing cab ride would give me the perfect opportunity to get my thoughts in order, since the very first thing I had to do in my new role was to address the entire company at nine o'clock sharp.

In hindsight, and given my knowledge of Sydney taxis, I can't believe I was so stupid. The problem turned out to be different from the usual "How do you get there?" variety. This time, the issue was a cabbie who wanted to talk. And, boy, could he talk.

He was totally impervious to any hint I gave him that I wanted to ride in silence.

"That's fascinating. I don't like Thatcher either, but if you don't mind I've got to prepare a speech, so please don't think I'm rude if I do some work now," I said after my fourth attempt to shut him up had failed.

"Oh. No worries, mate. I understand. Sometimes I get so busy myself that I just can't focus on anything else. Drives my missus crazy. Ha ha. Take tax return time. Do you fill out your own tax return?"

"Uh, yeah, but I've really got . . ."

"Me, too. I hate it. Always leave it to the last moment and then have to lock myself away without any distractions . . ."

And so he went on. Eventually I had to spell out that it wasn't that I didn't like him but that I didn't want to have a conversation and could he please not disturb me. Miraculously, he actually stopped talking, but instead—and here's where it all went wrong—he turned the radio on.

I am one of those people who can't get the last song they've heard on the radio in the morning out of their head all day. For this reason, when I'm working I only ever listen to news radio—never music—in the mornings on a weekday. This guy clearly didn't have the same philosophy—puerile pop music blasted out at deafening volume. My big mistake was hesitating before asking him to turn it off. After all, I had just said I didn't want to talk to him, so I felt a bit uncomfortable telling him he couldn't listen to the radio in his own car. By the time this thought process had come and gone the song had already caught hold of my brain.

"You and me, baby, we ain't nothing but mammals, so let's do it like they do on the Discovery Channel. You and me, baby, we ain't nothing but mammals, so let's do it like they do on the

Discovery Channel. You and me, baby, we ain't nothing but mammals, so let's do it like they do on the Discovery Channel," blasted out of the radio.

It might have been repetitive, but it sure as hell was catchy. When I arrived at my new office I was a lost cause.

"Good morning, Mr. Marsh. Welcome to Leo Burnett," the friendly and professional receptionist said.

I heard my mouth say "Morning" while my brain sang, "You and me, baby, we ain't nothing but mammals, so let's do it like they do on the Discovery Channel."

Todd was the second person to greet me. "Hi, Nige. They are all in the boardroom waiting for you," he said.

"You and me, baby, we ain't nothing but mammals, so let's do it like they do on the Discovery Channel," I replied.

"What?"

"Oh, nothing—have you heard that song?"

"Yeah—catchy, isn't it?"

"I'll say."

"Nige?"

"Yeah?"

"They are still all in the boardroom waiting for you," he repeated.

"Oh. Of course. I'll be right there," I replied. Walking up the stairs to the boardroom, I tried to focus myself, while all the while having to listen to the internal sound track of the mammal anthem.

It was all a bit surreal but I managed to get through the speech and the day satisfactorily. Unfortunately the rest of the week definitely wasn't satisfactory. Think Dunkirk without the boats. In my first meeting with the firm's second-largest client, they politely informed me that they were moving to a different agency. Visions of being fit, forty-one, and fired again flashed through my brain. It was my fourth day in the office and I was unprepared, to say the least. So unprepared, in fact, that I was wearing an England rugby shirt as it was the day of the opening ceremony of the Rugby World Cup, which I was attending later. (At least the rugby went according to plan—God bless you, Jonny Wilkinson.)

The moment they told me their decision I knew it meant I would have to lay off some of our employees. Some executives lose no sleep over doing this—they even relish the chance to prove their steeliness and seniority. Personally, taking away the livelihoods of colleagues is something that makes me ill. I can never quite rid myself of the notion that those who least deserve the bullet tend to get it, however hard you try to arrange matters more fairly.

Rather than a "steady as she goes" fact-finding start, my first month was spent telling people I was letting them go. I hate that phrase—it's almost as bad as the "I'm going to have to involuntarily separate you from the payroll system" euphemism apparently used in certain American firms. My brother tells me the army has a slightly more robust approach to such matters, "All those with a job take one pace forward . . . not so fast, Dickens," being an example he claims to have witnessed personally.

I tried to steer a middle course between British Army gallows humor and confusing American doublespeak as I delivered the bad news in a series of back-to-back meetings. But certain industry commentators were more blunt. One of the better head-lines from my early days back at work was "Bloodbath at House of Pain as New CEO Rips Guts Out of Once-Proud Agency."

Catchy though the song in the taxi had been, I felt more like an earthworm than a mammal by the end of my first month.

Chapter 51

Low Frequency

WORK WASN'T THE only cause for concern. My personal life started to fall apart.

For a start, I didn't do the Bondi to Bronte swim. For me this was devastating, not just because it was a goal I had been working toward for nine months, but more because my attempts to reinvent myself throughout the year had somehow come to be embodied by the race. Whenever I went for a training swim or even thought of the race, it reminded me of the broader goals I was working toward beyond completing the event itself. To not even enter the race therefore made me feel that I had failed completely.

It's not that I didn't want to do the race—I desperately did. My training had gone well and after completing a few cross–Bondi

Bay swims (there and back) I knew I was ready to do it. The trouble was work. My new firm's headquarters were in America and I had to attend a conference there on the weekend of the race. Sitting in Chicago on the morning the event was taking place in Sydney, it was difficult to put things into the proper perspective. To add insult to injury, at my next doctor's checkup, she told me all my training for the race had given me "swimmer's ear."

"What's that?" I asked.

"It's a common condition in Australia. It means there's a build-up—like the furring of a lead pipe—in your ear canal."

"And what does that mean?" I asked.

"Well, it impairs your hearing, I'm afraid. But luckily in your case it's only low-frequency sound that will be affected," she reassured me.

"Oh. Good. What's included in low-frequency sound?" I asked.

"Human speech, mainly," she replied.

Wonderful.

Beyond the race, there were many other areas of failure. A key part of my written personal contract was an agreement with Kate that every Wednesday night would be "date night." This was to be the evening where, irrespective of work and career pressures, I would drop everything and go out with Kate. This commitment was devised not just as an end in itself (i.e., a good night out), but it was an important means to an end as well. It would be a way of helping me keep tabs on my work-life balance, because if I couldn't take one night a week off, then I would know I was losing the plot. Twelve weeks into the job, I hadn't been able to get away once. Not once. Twelve dates in a row canceled. Lovely.

On top of the canceled personal time I was soon bringing my work home and tormenting Kate with the travails of the job. Déjà vu all over again. I was also starting to shout at the kids again. One morning during my second week back, I actually managed to make all four of them cry before Kate woke up—a bizarre personal achievement for someone who was supposed to have changed his outlook on life in general and family in particular.

I was struggling. To top things off nicely, just when I thought things couldn't get worse I read an article in the *Sydney Morning Herald* that quoted the former CEO of Microsoft in Australia. I'd never met Daniel Petre but it was like he was warning me personally when I read his opinion on the life CEOs lead: "They have no friends other than work; they have no relationships with their spouse; their kids don't care about them; they have no hobbies. They lead very insular, single-dimension lives and they don't have the courage to admit it."

Sugar the pill, why don't you.

Chapter 52

Winegums

A WHOLE GENERATION OF women has long since realized that the "You can have it all" dream was just that—a dream. This is a lesson that seems to have been lost on men so we're still trying to achieve it. There is a mountain of literature advising men on how to achieve work-life balance, and I believe that not only is this advice misguided, it is also part of the problem.

Stressed executives all over the developed world now have the added stress of trying to do it all. All our striving for balance is making us less balanced, not more. The bar has been set at a completely unrealistic level. Many men try desperately hard to do it all—and then beat themselves up when they aren't home for their kids' suppers. When they do finally get home, they feel like failures and deal with their frustration by being morose and shouting at the wife and kids. (Well, that's what I was doing.)

For a while in the 1990s, it was like a collective madness had taken hold. No one had the sense or guts to ask, "If it didn't work for women in the 1980s, why on earth do we think it will work for men now?" Instead, a whole host of commentators gave the message that with a few compromises, men *could* have it all.

If you think some of the old *Cosmo* articles advising women to have the best of both worlds by staying in the office all night and faxing their orgasms to their husbands are funny, you should read some of the bullshit written by so-called experts about fathers. Most display a complete lack of understanding about the economic, family, and business realities that 99 percent of us have to live with. No one will admit it, but just like employers avoid employing women who might get pregnant soon, they also don't want men who genuinely have a balanced life. They want the job done well and they know that doing something important well demands a person's full investment. When it comes down to shareholders, your marriage and the school cafeteria can go screw themselves.

There are signs that although the situation isn't necessarily improving, a more honest debate about it is starting to happen. The business magazine *Fast Company* led with the front cover splash "Balance Is Bunk!" in its October 2004 issue, with an article calling the idea of work-life balance fatally flawed and discussing the central myth of the modern workplace: "The truth is, balance is bunk. It is an unattainable pipe dream, a vain artifice that offers mostly rhetorical solutions to problems of logistics and economics. The quest for balance between work and life, as we've come to think of it, isn't just a losing proposition; it's a hurtful, destructive one," read the article.

However, the debate has also got to be honest on an individual level. There's no point in me going on about comfortable generalities if when it comes down to it I then kid myself about my own real feelings toward the office.

I have a confession—looking after four young children isn't always as rewarding as performing well in a business meeting. It *is* sometimes fantastic to be able to leave the domestic chores behind and go on a business trip. I *do* get a large part of my identity from my role at work. I find it enormously satisfying and motivating to be part of a group of people that is engaged in common endeavor toward a shared goal—even when that goal is business success. No, that last sentence is dishonest: *especially* when that goal is business success. I like hard work. Nothing worthwhile is ever easy. I'm competitive and find winning a thrill—not at all costs, but I am prepared to make personal sacrifices to achieve commercial victory. I mean look at me: I didn't even last a year before I traded in arsenic hour for the business lounge.

So am I recommending that all men just give up trying to lead more balanced lives? No. I'm not recommending anything. I haven't got any answers. I do, however, look at things in a different way now. I have stopped looking for perfection. Having spent my life so far seeing only black and white, I am now more comfortable with gray.

Life is hard, and as far as I can see it will always be hard. The vast majority of us will *always* have to struggle—whatever lifestyle choices we make. Admitting this to myself was liberating in its own right. I then started to focus on enjoying the struggle rather than attempting to create a mythical stress-free nirvana. I've started to praise myself for the small victories rather than beat myself up for the bigger failure of not having a perfect life.

Now every time one of the kids does something gorgeous, instead of descending into a pit of despair that I'm missing all the *other* gorgeous moments, I count myself lucky that I was present for that one. I'm grateful for every time I manage to drive the kids to school rather than resentful for those times that I can't. I'm basically working on the habit of counting my blessings, not whining about the challenges.

I may be struggling, but the struggle is slightly more enjoyable and less damaging to those around me than it was a year ago. The contrast between the two Christmas holidays on either side of my almost-year off couldn't be more dramatic. Admittedly, I didn't have to wear paper pants for the second one, but I was working just as hard, if not harder. Yet despite the work pressures I had the most magical family time.

Harry was full of surprises, as usual: On top of his list for Santa he wrote "a big warm blankit." When Kate asked him about this request he said he had been cold all year. Along with the problem of it being rectangular in shape, no wonder he didn't like his bed.

Eve was unbelievably proud that people kept on talking about "Christmas Eve," which meant Grace walked around telling everyone she was "Christmas Grace." One of their presents was a video of *The Sound of Music* so I spent half the time being forced to whistle and then watch as the girls stood to attention shoulder to shoulder before marching around the house. (Unfortunately this didn't last.) When I asked Alex if he had had a nice Christmas he looked at me and replied, "Dad, it was great. I'm only eight and I've already got so many good memories." There were arguments, of course, but even they were wonderful in their own special way.

On Boxing Day, Grace came running into our bedroom in a flood of tears. When we asked her what was wrong she held up her right hand so the palm was facing us and sobbed, "I showed Eve the stop sign but she kept doing it!" She said this in a tone of stunned amazement that the "stop sign" hadn't worked. Apparently they had just learned this technique in preschool.

I bow to their superior child-rearing skills, but they will have to come up with something slightly more effective to stop Eve from hitting her sister. When I sternly lectured Eve for this "unacceptable behavior" her bottom lip quivered and she ran into our bedroom to tell Kate, "Mommy, Daddy's hurt my feelings!" Peace resumed a few minutes later and without warning Eve came up behind me, put her arms around my neck, and whispered into my ear, "Daddy, I love you all around the Harbor Bridge much." Not quite sure what it meant, but it will do for me.

Encouragingly, the successes weren't just confined to Christmas. I'm still sober, not having touched a drop since April 2003. I am trim—no six-pack yet but definitely still trim. The bond with my children has been permanently improved. Harry continues to use his real name; Grace has ceased to torment me in public. I not only took Alex to a number of the rugby World Cup games, but I have also done another Lads and Dad trip—this time camping in the bush for a weekend. I entered and completed not one but three ocean races in 2004. I've kept up my running and even started to go for runs with Alex in the morning before work. I no longer sit in the car outside the house after work. Most important of all, Kate continues to put up with me.

Of course, I continue to be a deeply flawed executive, father, and husband but I have no doubt that my year off was more than just an extended vacation—it started me on a personal journey. I have no illusions of ever arriving at a final destination but I am deeply committed to sticking with it, wherever it may lead. This may be to completely surprising places, as almost every week teaches me something wholly unexpected. A recent revelation seems a fitting point to end the story.

It happened while I was on a hike with my brother, Jon, and cousin Clive at a recent family reunion in the U.K. We were going to be walking all day and had each agreed to bring some sweets and chocolate to keep us going. On the way to meet them I stopped at a garage to fill up the car with gas. When I went to pay, I was delighted to notice that some bright marketing genius had finally gotten around to releasing red and black winegums.

Winegums, or gummy bears, as I'm told they are called in America, were my favorite childhood sweet and to this day I still buy them when going on long car journeys or walks. Trouble was, for every packet I bought, I always had to eat ten or so bloody green, orange, and yellow ones just to get to the one or two red and black ones.

Now, everyone knows that the best winegums are the red and black ones. No one prefers the orange, green, or yellow ones. At best they are tolerated—never looked forward to or savored. A whole pack of *just* red and black ones was almost too good to be true. It's the confectionary equivalent of your wife saying, "I thought tonight I'd surprise you with the nurse's uniform and suspenders. Don't worry about me, I just want to do all those things you mention when you're drunk that we've not got around to doing yet." I was so delighted with my discovery that I bought the entire stock—seventeen packets, to be precise. We were definitely going to have enough energy on the walk.

Jon and Clive shared my excitement when I showed them my confectionary gold mine. But the weirdest thing happened on the walk. To start with, we munched our way through the packets with gusto. Then, after a couple of miles hiking, we all simply stopped eating them. We ate some chocolate instead or drank water. I still had twelve packets of red and black winegums in my backpack at the end of the day, despite running out of all other snacks. The truth hit me on the drive home. The reason I used to like red and black winegums so much was *because* of the orange, green, and yellow ones.

Which, I suppose, is the point. You've got to be careful what you wish for in life. It may not turn out to be as wonderful as the fantasy. With the right attitude, the bad bits aren't always that bad and indeed most of the time they are the very reason you actually enjoy the good times. I may be struggling back at work but I'm happy with the struggle, I'm happy with the year off, and I'm happy with the year ahead. Struggle and all.

Which is not to say I wouldn't appreciate a bit more involvement on the suspenders and nurse's uniform front . . .

Acknowledgments

A NUMBER OF PEOPLE were enormously encouraging and helpful during the process of writing and publishing this book. I would like to thank:

Tara Wynne, Jude McGee, Jessica Dettmann, Faye Bender, Kirsty Melville and Chris Schillig and all the others who helped at Andrews McMeel, Claudia and Jonathon Crow, Vickie and Miles, Paul Wilson, Bill Ford, Katie and James, Charlie Lawrence, Hugh Mackay, Justin and Jacqi, David Rollins, Miche Holdsworth, David Holtham, Ilona Levchenko, Jane and Max, Peter Giutronich, Tom Loewy, Margaret Marsh, and, of course, the tea bag beacher herself, my darling wife, Kate.

I would also like to thank everyone who worked at D'Arcy Australia and all of my colleagues at Leo Burnett Australia—two very special groups of individuals. I feel privileged to have been a part of each team.

Alcoholics Anonymous can be contacted via its Web site, www.aa.org, or by looking in your phone book for the nearest meeting.

To contact the author, go to www.fatfortyandfired.com.